HARRY HOUDINI for KIDS

HIS LIFE AND ADVENTURES

WITH 21 MAGIC TRICKS AND ILLUSIONS

LAURIE CARLSON

CHICAGO
REVIEW
PRESS

Library of Congress Cataloging-in-Publication Data

Carlson, Laurie M., 1952–

    Harry Houdini for kids : his life and adventures
with 21 magic tricks and illusions / Laurie Carlson.
— 1st ed.

      p. cm.

      Includes index.

      ISBN 978-1-55652-782-1 (pbk.)

      1. Houdini, Harry, 1874–1926—Juvenile
literature. 2. Magicians—United States—
Biography—Juvenile literature. 3. Escape artists—
United States—Biography—Juvenile literature.
4. Magic tricks. I. Title.

    GV1545.H8C33 2009

    793.8092—dc22

    [B]

                    2008021404

Cover and interior design: Joan Sommers Design
Cover image credits: (Left to right) Busch Circus
poster, c. 1912. Postcard of the Hippodrome, New
York; Private collection. Houdini, bound and chained
to a large metal wheel; Photograph courtesy of the
Walter P. Reuther Library, Wayne State University.
Harry Houdini; Photograph courtesy of the Library
of Congress, LC-USZC4-3277.

Published by Chicago Review Press, Incorporated
814 North Franklin Street
Chicago, Illinois 60610
978-1-55652-782-1
Printed in Italy
5 4 3 2 1

TO BRIAN AND TYLER,
BOYS WITH BIG IDEAS
AND ENERGY TO MATCH.

CONTENTS

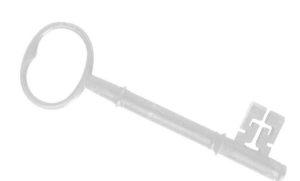

TIME LINE

1874 Ehrich Weisz born in Budapest, Hungary

1878 Weisz family moves to Appleton, Wisconsin, changes name to Weiss

1887 Weiss family moves to New York City

1891 Ehrich joins with a friend to create a magic act: the Houdini Brothers. He begins using the name Harry Houdini.

1892 Harry's father dies

1893 Harry's brother Dash replaces friend in the Houdini Brothers; they perform at Chicago World's Fair

1893 Harry marries Bess Rahner after knowing her for three weeks

1893 Harry and Bess, now "The Houdinis," spend six years struggling with their act

1899 Houdinis get a big break, perform in top vaudeville theaters across the country

1900 Houdinis tour Britain and Europe

1905 Houdinis return to United States and buy a house in New York City and a small farm in Connecticut

1907 Harry begins doing handcuffed bridge jumps

HARRY HOUDINI THE JAIL BREAKER
INTRODUCING HIS LATEST & GREATEST
PRISON CELL & BARREL MYSTERY

1908 Harry does the Milk Can Escape

1910 Harry is the first person to fly an airplane in Australia—he spends three and a half minutes in the air

1912 Harry does the Chinese Water Torture Cell stunt

1914 World War I begins

1918 Harry does the Vanishing Elephant act as part of a large extravaganza marking the end of World War I

1919 Harry becomes a movie star when *The Master Mystery* opens in theaters

1920 The Funk and Wagnalls dictionary includes the word *houdinize*, which means "to release or extricate oneself from (confinement, bonds, or the like), as by wriggling out"

1922 Houdini begins investigating spirit mediums

1926 In February Harry testifies before a congressional committee investigating paranormal frauds or anyone pretending to tell fortunes for money

In October while at McGill University in Montreal, Canada, Harry is punched hard in the stomach. He becomes ill and a few days later has his appendix removed. After another surgery, he dies on October 31 in Detroit, Michigan.

2002 U.S. Postal Service issues a first-class commemorative stamp honoring Houdini

Houdini returned in 2002—
on a postage stamp!
U. S. POSTAL SERVICE

vii

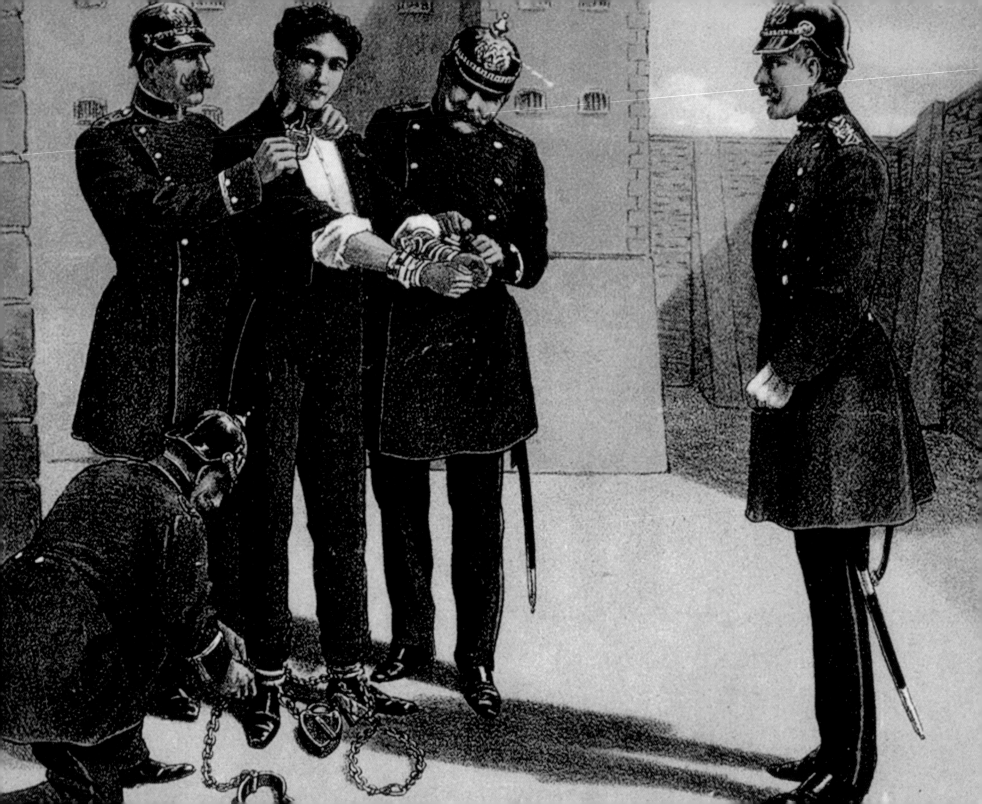

INTRODUCTION

Houdini created Houdini. When considering the life of Ehrich Weisz, who would become the great Harry Houdini, it's important to note that some stories he told have been contradicted and that he often "re-created" his past for personal reasons. His birth date, birthplace, childhood, and other details were often changed. In the late 1800s Jewish immigrants faced discrimination in the United States, a condition that worsened as Houdini came to adulthood and led him to smooth over his foreign roots. As a child, he was reared in a household where no English was spoken—his parents spoke German. When touring in Europe, he taught himself to speak other languages so he could better connect with the audience, and his childhood German came in handy. He also dabbled in speaking French, Russian, and Danish. But his allegiance was never in question. After World War I began, he found himself more determined than ever to be recognized as a solid citizen of the United States.

In many ways Houdini's rise to fame was a result of the conditions that existed during the era in which he lived. The country faced internal divisions and bitter conflicts between employees and employers. Urban tenements were packed with frustrated people, immigrants continued arriving, and the country was in turmoil as labor unions expanded and pressed for a better quality of life. Parades, protests, and riots were common. Crowds gathered in the streets for a variety of reasons, and for Houdini, entertaining the mob grew naturally out of the circumstances. He would do a stunt as thousands gathered in the street below, watching for hours—something the public happily engaged in before moving

pictures and other forms of entertainment were invented. People were also eager to visit inexpensive circus sideshows and cheap amusements, which allowed people like Houdini to make a living from their unusual or quirky talents.

As a kid, Harry Houdini began with card tricks and simple magic acts. Gradually he developed his talents as an escape artist, which became his signature act. He dared anyone to come up with something he couldn't escape. Working against ropes, handcuffs, or whatever contraption at hand, he always wriggled loose somehow. People loved it! A lone individual against powerful forces emerging free through his own wits and strength was very popular.

His career really grew in Europe, where he worked for five years. The people loved him, especially in Russia and Germany, which were countries with stiff police control over the citizenry. People thrilled to see an ordinary fellow escape handcuffs and restraints. Houdini returned to the United States, where he marketed himself and his stunts to a wide audience.

Houdini created his acts and stunts carefully, in some cases preparing and practicing them for years before ever performing them publicly. He took pride in figuring out how to fool people, knowing they wanted to be fooled as part of the fun. But because he did such seemingly impossible stunts, such as escaping several sets of handcuffs and ropes after jumping off a bridge into a flowing river, some people claimed he had supernatural powers. For a time, many believed he could disintegrate and take other physical forms. He hated that—he didn't want people to think his talent was due to a spirit; he wanted them to respect his cleverness at creating and perfecting the trick or illusion.

That made him begin debunking those who claimed to have supernatural powers, such as Spiritualists and mediums. He also revealed the secrets of those who used tricks to do wrong, such as criminals. He even exposed some of his competitors who tried to make a living copying his act. By working hard to expose and explain the history of magic, he was turning it into a respectable profession. He knew magicians had influenced and entertained people for thousands of years, and he wanted to

chronicle magicians of the past to gain prestige for magicians in the present. He created a magicians' guild, the Society of American Magicians (SAM), becoming its first president. He wanted to be remembered as a solidly professional magician.

Houdini was unique. Although his education was sparse, since he had been forced to go to work as a child, his greatest joy was his book collection—numbering thousands of volumes—and he even wrote several books himself. Like many other children at the time, he turned to the public library for an education, reading everything he could find that would help him achieve his goals.

His life shows how creativity, perseverance, and resilience can overcome setbacks and lack of opportunity. Houdini was an immigrant street kid who became such a popular success that his name entered the dictionary during his lifetime, and his life was later celebrated with a U.S. postage stamp. Today, decades after his death and a century after he became popular, Houdini remains fascinating.

Humble Beginnings

On March 24, 1874, Ehrich Weisz, the boy who grew up to reinvent himself as Harry Houdini, was born in Budapest, Hungary. His parents quickly had a houseful—they already had three older sons, and another son was born after Ehrich. Their father, Mayer Samuel Weisz, had studied to be a lawyer, but he found little opportunity in Hungary. The family was just getting by and times looked bleak. They were Jewish and many Jews in Europe suffered discrimination and harsh treatment. Like many other immigrants from Europe at that time, Mayer Weisz booked passage on a ship to New York City.

COMING TO AMERICA

In the late 1800s millions of immigrants came to the United States from Eastern and Southern Europe. They arrived by ship, usually traveling in family groups, with everything they owned tied in bundles or trunks. Industrialization in Europe meant that machinery replaced human labor, leaving many people without jobs or farmland. In Russia, masses of Jews left to avoid harsh anti-Jewish government policies. Over 23 million immigrants entered the United States between 1880 and 1920. From 1900 to 1914, a million immigrants arrived every year.

When immigrants got off the ships in the New York harbor, health officers examined them. If they had signs of contagious diseases, they were quarantined, hospitalized, or sent back to Europe. The newcomers stayed in hotels and boardinghouses until they could get settled. Those with money headed west by train to find farmland. The West opened to settlers after the Civil War, and homesteaders could find land of their own along the new railroad lines. Those who were poor stayed in New York City, looking for work there at factory jobs. In 1879 almost half of the 180,000 immigrants who arrived in New York City stayed there. The rest headed by train to Wisconsin, Minnesota, Illinois, and Missouri.

This was the path followed by the Weisz family. After arriving in New York City, Mayer Weisz sent for his wife, Cecilia, and their five children. Ehrich was four years old. Cecilia and the boys traveled from the port of Hamburg, Germany, to New York City. It took them 15 days. They arrived the day before the Fourth of July and a stifling 95-degree heat wave.

Hungarian Jewish immigrants, like many others, typically changed their names when they entered the United States, Americanizing them to make them easier for English speakers to pronounce. The Weisz family changed their last name to Weiss. Armin became Herman; Natan became Nathan; Vilmos changed to William; Ehrich changed his to simply Erik, and the youngest, Deszo, became Theo—but they called him Dash. For Ehrich, it wouldn't be the last time he changed his name.

By that fall, the family was living in Appleton, Wisconsin, where Mayer had

found a house and job. Appleton was a small but growing town of 7,000 residents. Grain mills ground wheat into flour, and sawmills turned white pine into paper pulp. There were only about 75 Jewish people in the town, but they planned to build a synagogue and hired Mayer to serve as their rabbi. He was respected because he was highly educated and spoke several languages—Hebrew,

A magazine printed this image of immigrants getting off ships in New York in 1880.
HARPER'S WEEKLY, 1880

5

Immigrants heading to the train station with piles of belongings. They will head west.

HARPER'S WEEKLY, 1873

people, who replaced him four years later with a more modern-thinking rabbi. Or at least one who spoke English, which Rabbi Weiss did not. With no money and seven children, the Weisses moved to the nearest city, Milwaukee, to make a go of it. There the children went to work, finding whatever ways to earn money they could. Ehrich bought newspapers and resold them on the streets, polished men's boots for a few cents, or ran errands. They were destitute, and Cecilia had to go to the Hebrew Relief Society to ask for food for the children and coal to heat the house.

One day Ehrich and his younger brother Dash lost nearly their entire day's earnings—two dollars—on the way home. To make up for the loss, Ehrich used their remaining nickel to buy a flower from a florist shop. He went out on the street and sold the flower to a passerby for ten cents—doubling his investment. Dash joined him and the two bought and sold flowers until they had recovered two dollars. They hurried home, knowing their mother wouldn't be disappointed.

When he was nine, Ehrich joined an older kid who started the Jack Hoeffler 5-Cent Circus to make money. Ehrich created a tightrope stunt, calling himself

Hungarian, and German—and wrote poetry and essays. The family became U.S. citizens and added two more children: another son, Leopold, and finally a daughter, Gladys.

EHRICH GOES TO WORK
Rabbi Weiss was a serious, studious man, far too serious, it seems, for the Appleton

Ehrich, Prince of the Air, after seeing a traveling tightrope walker. The young people performed in an open field, Ehrich swinging from ropes and doing acrobatic stunts wearing a pair of red knitted tights his mother made for him. His first stunt? Bending over backward and picking a pin up off the ground with his teeth. Later he claimed he also picked up sewing pins from the floor with his eyelashes—but no one can know for sure.

Houdini later remembered, "Training as a contortionist was, of course, the first step toward my present occupation of escaping from strait-jackets and chains, for it is chiefly through my ability to twist my body and dislocate my joints, together with abnormal expansion and contraction powers, which renders me independent of the tightest bonds." Gymnastics, exercise, and tumbling would remain part of his physical fitness training for the rest of his life.

His interests moved from gymnastics and acrobatics to magic. He had to teach himself, however, turning to books for all the information he could devour. He spent plenty of time at the public library reading whatever books caught his interest. His first book purchase, for ten cents, was a simple little book about magic.

Many children had to work instead of attending school.
LIBRARY OF CONGRESS, LC-DIG-NCK-05195, LC-D401-11590

Step Through a Note Card

It took many years and lots of hard work before Harry Houdini became famous—or even well paid. As a kid he began doing street tricks, card tricks, and other sorts of things to earn tips from passersby. Those simple but clever little tricks remained important to him throughout the rest of his career because he often had to come up with something quickly to capture attention and interest. Here's a clever trick with a note card that he described in his book *Houdini's Paper Magic*.

The secret to this trick, or any magic trick, is in the presentation. Before performing, be sure to get the audience interested, stoking their curiosity with your enthusiasm. "Now . . . laaadies and geeentlemen . . . I will step through this note card, yes, this simple note card (pass it around for them to look over). With just a few snips from a pair of ordinary scissors, I'll show you how it's done!"

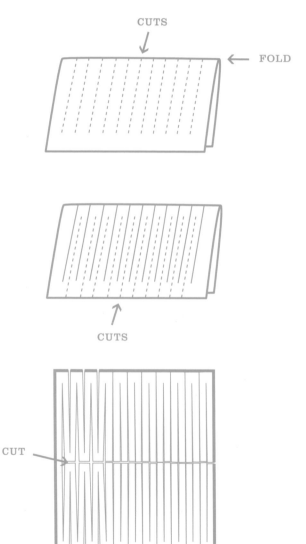

CUTS

FOLD

CUTS

CUT

MATERIALS

1 index card (You might want to try the trick with a larger paper rectangle—it will work just fine, too, and will be easier to step through.)

Scissors

Fold the card lengthwise down the center. Using the scissors, make a series of cuts about 1/8-inch apart, cutting through the fold and stopping about 1/4-inch from the edge. After you've made cuts across the entire card, turn to the other side and make another series of cuts, beginning along the edge and cutting just up to the fold. Make the cuts in between the earlier cuts. Unfold the card, spreading it flat. Leaving the first and last sections uncut, cut straight across through the fold. Gently expand the card and you'll have a stretchy, flexible paper chain you can slip over your head and on over your body, stepping through it to audience applause.

Street magic—simple tricks done with papers, coins, or marbles—was easy for Ehrich to learn and cost nothing. It's always fun to learn some of the simple tricks he read about and practiced.

Even with the children working, the Weiss family was not able to make enough money to support themselves. When Ehrich was 11 years old, his parents sent him back to Appleton, hoping he could learn a skill to earn better pay. Ehrich lived with and worked as an apprentice to Mr. Hanauer, a locksmith in Appleton. Locks and hardware had always fascinated Ehrich. When he was younger he had used a wire buttonhook (a tool for buttoning ladies' boots) to open locked cabinets at home. He had also surprised the neighborhood in Appleton by somehow unlocking all the doors on College Avenue one night. Now, under Mr. Hanauer's guidance, he taught himself exactly how locks worked. When an opportunity arose to show off his talent, he discovered his unique skill might one day be important.

A policeman brought a handcuffed prisoner to the lock shop one day. The fellow had been found innocent and the police wanted to release him, but the key to the lock had broken off inside the lock. Mr. Hanauer and the officer went out for

CHILD LABOR

As the United States became more industrial, factories needed workers, and children were sometimes sent to fill the need. Mines, too, employed children as workers. By the end of the 1800s, the nation was beginning to worry that children were working too much and not attending school.

The Progressive Movement in the early 20th century pushed to get children into school instead of factories and mines. It was difficult because states were in charge of labor laws. Efforts to create an amendment to the U.S. Constitution to protect children from overwork were repeatedly defeated. In 1938 Congress finally passed the Fair Labor Standards Act, which prohibited child labor in the manufacturing of goods sold in other states and restricted children between 16 and 18 years from some dangerous jobs.

Ehrich attended very little school. His parents were educated: his mother could speak five languages and his father had a large collection of books. Some of his brothers went to school—one even became a physician—but Ehrich spent his time working, educating himself by reading whenever he could.

a snack, leaving Ehrich to figure out the task. After several futile attempts to saw the handcuffs apart, Ehrich decided to use a secret technique for opening the cuffs' lock—one he'd discovered himself. He took a pick, inserted it into the lock's mechanism, and with a few twists the locked cuffs sprang open.

Mr. Hanauer returned to the shop in time to see the open handcuffs lying on the table. He saw they hadn't been sawed apart

Odd Number Trick

This is the sort of magic trick that makes people think you have some sort of extrasensory perception, or ESP. Houdini enjoyed performing these kinds of tricks, but he also wanted people to realize it was just a well-developed trick because he wanted them to respect his intelligence and hard work. He didn't want them to think he was relying on extrasensory powers or spirits.

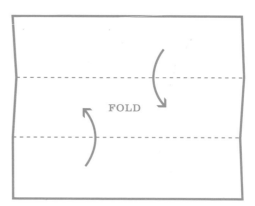

MATERIALS

- 1 sheet writing paper
- Pens or pencils for everyone
- 9 people to participate

Before you start, show everyone you're using an ordinary blank sheet of paper. Ask them to inspect the paper to see that nothing has been written on it. Then fold the paper in thirds, then thirds again. Open and tear the paper along the folds, creating nine pieces. You'll see that only one of the pieces is torn along all four edges. Pass the papers out to the participants, remembering which person you gave that piece to. Ask that person to

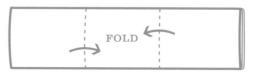

write down an odd number. Ask the rest to write down even numbers and fold the papers in half. Collect them in a hat or in a pile on a table. You'll be able to use your "mental magic powers" to select the one paper with the odd number on it from the pile. Remember, it's the one with the torn edges all the way around.

Another version of this trick is called The Living and the Dead. The magician asks the person receiving the paper with the four torn edges to write down the name of George Washington, while others write the names of living people. Selecting the "dead" (George Washington) is easy!

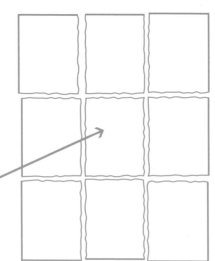

Tear along the folds. Only the center one will have four torn edges

or broken. "That's very good work," he told Ehrich. At that point, Ehrich realized he might find his special talent useful someday. He didn't know that handcuff escape acts would make him an international star.

Years later Harry Houdini remembered that day, saying, "The very manner in which I then picked the lock of the handcuff contained the basic principle which I employed in opening handcuffs all over the world. *Not with a duplicate key*, which seems to have been the only way others had of duplicating my performance." The prisoner remained the only person ever to watch Houdini open a lock. We still don't know his secret.

But working in the shop didn't last long, and Ehrich returned to his family in Milwaukee. About that time, at the age of 12, he ended up striking out on his own. He rode a train toward Texas looking for opportunity but somehow ended up in Kansas City, Missouri. Boarding another train, he wound up back in Wisconsin, about 50 miles from his family. For unknown reasons he didn't return to his family at that time. A childless couple, the Flitcrofts, took him in and cared for him that summer.

In 1887 Ehrich rejoined his father and the two ended up in New York City, hoping to find work and a new home for the rest of the family. They lived in a boardinghouse for a time. Mayer sold some of his book collection to buy food, and the rest of the family soon joined them.

Again Ehrich and his brothers tried to make money by doing odd jobs as well as using their wits. Ehrich worked the sidewalks, doing card tricks and magic tricks for donations. Rabbi Weiss, who worked cutting out clothing for a sweatshop, was often ill and knew the family was in dire straits. One day he made Ehrich promise to take care of Cecilia for the rest of her life if anything happened to Mayer. Ehrich didn't hesitate. Of course he would, he told his father. Like most children, he figured that day would never come.

When Ehrich noticed a sign outside a shop saying Help Wanted, he perked up. There was a long line of applicants standing outside the door, waiting to apply. Ehrich, desperate for something to support the family, rushed up to the front, brashly took down the sign, and went inside the front door.

"I'm here for the job," he told the surprised clerk. That was enough—he got the job and went to work immediately, cutting fabric into strips for others to stitch into neckties.

"An old trick well done is far better than a new trick with no effect."

—HOUDINI

A Star Is Born

Ehrich's brash confidence helped him get the job at Richter's necktie factory and was a key to his success. He had nothing to lose and needed the work and the money desperately, so he didn't feel he could hang back and wait to be noticed. Getting noticed and making a name for himself would be a goal throughout his life.

SPORTS AND FITNESS

For a young person with little money or opportunities, sports offered a chance to become a winner. Ehrich could work out and train without spending much money, then compete, win prizes, and gain attention and acceptance. He excelled at many sports, including running and swimming. He trained by swimming in the East River and jogging a ten-mile run through Central Park.

Ehrich joined an athletic club, the Pastime Athletic Club, where he could make friends and enter competitions. He became so good that he tried out for the U.S. Olympic swim team, but he didn't make it. At age 16 he won a prize in the American Amateur Athletic Union one-mile race, and at 18 he set a record for a run around Central Park and defeated an English champion in a 20-mile race.

Ehrich also enjoyed gymnastics, and in New York he began learning to box. By age 17 he was good enough to compete in amateur boxing matches, aiming for the 115-pound championship, which could have launched him in a boxing career. He became ill, however, and couldn't complete the finals. The boy who won the championship had already lost to Ehrich in an earlier bout, so Ehrich might have won the match.

In addition to excelling at running, swimming, and boxing, Erich was an avid cyclist. Bicycle racing was a popular sport at the time, and Ehrich kept a scrapbook filled with newspaper stories about the winning bicyclists. He used a bicycle often himself, both to keep in shape and for transportation. He worked as a bicycle messenger, delivering messages around the city.

Keeping his body in top shape laid the foundation for Ehrich's later career, and he always prided himself on his strength and agility. He refused to use alcohol or smoke cigarettes, partly because his father had forbid them as immoral and partly because his coach at the Pastime Athletic Club warned him they would ruin his athletic ability.

HARRY HOUDINI IS BORN

Ehrich had always been interested in magic tricks and stunts, and he amused friends at the athletic club and the necktie factory with clever card and coin tricks. He performed in the neighborhood at places like the Young Men's Hebrew Association, where he called himself Ehrich the Great. Without money to buy equipment, however, his act was limited to simple tricks. Then, when he was about

15 years old, he discovered a book that changed his life. It was called *Memoirs of Robert-Houdin, Ambassador, Author, and Conjurer, Written by Himself*. He stayed up all night reading the book about Robert-Houdin, then the world's most famous magician. It was also a book about magic, a topic Ehrich utterly fell in love with. Robert-Houdin, a French magician, recorded his adventurous life as a performing magician during the middle 1800s. His stories of performing illusions involving people floating in the air, as well as performances before European kings and queens, fascinated Ehrich.

Ehrich's mother found him the next morning, still in his work clothes, pouring through the pages of the book. The book became a foundation for the rest of his life. He said, "My interest in conjuring and magic and my enthusiasm for Robert-Houdin came into existence simultaneously. From the moment that I began to study the art, he became my guide and hero. I accepted his writings as my textbook and my gospel." It sparked his interest in magic as a professional career. "To my unsophisticated mind, his 'Memoirs' gave to the profession a dignity worth attaining at the cost of earnest, life-long effort," he said.

Ehrich, about 16 years old, shows off medals he won in track competitions.

Linking Paper Rings

Here's a trick Houdini wrote about in his book *Paper Magic*. It's based on a mathematical discovery made in 1858. You'll take three "ordinary" paper loops and cut them to create five loops while your audience watches.

MATERIALS

> 1 large newspaper sheet
>
> Scissors
>
> Tape

Cut three long newspaper strips of the same length, each 2 inches wide. Tape the ends to make three rings. Tape the first ring with ends overlapped. When taping the second strip, give the paper a single twist before taping the ends. For the third ring, give the paper end two twists before taping the ends. A casual observer won't notice they are different.

Now for the effect. Cut down the center of the first ring, to make two rings exactly alike (A).

Cut down the center of the second ring and voila! You've made one ring, twice as long as the first (B).

Cut down the center of the third ring and you'll have two interlocking loops (C).

When you twisted the paper before joining the ends, you created a mobius strip—it has no boundary point between the inside and outside of the strip. Mobius strips are used as conveyor belts and typewriter printer ribbons. All sides of the strip get equal wear, so it lasts longer.

A   B   C

From that book on, Ehrich began collecting all the information he could find or afford regarding magic. Eventually he built a huge personal library that helped him research stunts, tricks, and the history of magic. At about this time, Ehrich also began taking acting and debate courses at a local club, hoping to polish his ability to speak and present before an audience.

In 1891, while working at Richter's, 17-year-old Ehrich and a fellow necktie cutter, Jacob Hyman, joined to create a magic act to bring in extra money. Ehrich called himself Ehrich the Great, or Cardo if he was doing card tricks. Jacob changed his name to Jack Hayman. The pair realized they needed a better, more theatrical stage name, but what?

Ehrich wanted to emulate his newly discovered hero, Robert-Houdin. Jacob told Ehrich that if you added the letter *i* to a person's name in French, it meant "like" that person. Certainly, being like Robert-Houdin was Ehrich's goal. *Houdin* with an *i* became *Houdini*, and Ehrich, who had been given the nickname Ehrie by family members, became Harry. At that moment Ehrich's new identity and name came together, and he became Harry Houdini.

Harry and Jack called themselves the Houdini Brothers. They did simple acts such as card tricks, coin swaps, and disappearing scarves that reappeared as flowers, as well as a trunk escape trick that didn't take expensive props or equipment. It wasn't easy getting bookings, however. Harry took the plunge and quit his job at Richter's, doing solo acts when Jack couldn't join him.

In 1892, at nearly the same time Harry was launching his magic career, his father fell seriously ill. Rabbi Weiss had cancer and knew he was dying. He called Harry to his bedside and made Harry promise to take care of his mother. Harry had already made that promise to his father when he was 12 years old. Now he repeated it as the old man faded away. How Harry would support his mother without an education or trade was not clear. But he vowed to fulfill the promise.

Harry set out to perform as often as possible, scraping for whatever he could earn by his wits. He got a gig at Huber's Dime Museum, where he performed with a series of freaks, strong men, and variety acts. Dime museums were a lot like circus sideshows, but remained in one place. Instead of the show traveling from town to town, the freaks and performers traveled between dime museums. For Harry, it was starting at the bottom of show business, but he could make steady money and learn the tricks of the trade from the other performers.

Harry also got hired at Coney Island's amusement park, where he worked in a tent with a strongman, passing the hat between acts for audience donations. Coney Island was popular with New Yorkers trying to escape the heat of the city during the summer. The beach was full of swimmers and the boardwalk was full of sideshow acts and food vendors. It was not a much better situation than dime museums or circus sideshows for the Houdini Brothers, but it was a job.

Harry needed to add to the act if he wanted to gain better bookings in higher-class places where audiences paid more for the show. He needed more magic tricks, but tricks cost money. Magic tricks, like other creative works, can be protected from copying by others by filing for copyright protection with the U.S. government. Magicians can copyright their original tricks; then, when they get tired of performing that trick (or need the cash) they can sell the rights to do the trick to someone else. Houdini, like other magicians, bought acts and tricks

Dime museums featured human freaks, animal acts, and other attractions. Houdini and others got their show business start in dime museums.

HARPER'S WEEKLY, 1881. IN *NEW YORK IN THE NINETEENTH CENTURY*, DOVER PUBLICATIONS, 1977

DIME MUSEUMS

Paying to see unusual-looking people began in Europe during the Middle Ages, when individuals traveled to country fairs to exhibit themselves. In the American colonies, roving showmen traveled from town to town, exhibiting unusual people or exotic animals no one had seen before, such as a lion or elephant. They were called curiosities, and people who looked unusual or had some unique physical condition (or could fake one) were called human curiosities.

In the 1700s and early 1800s such curiosities were shown in the first museums, along with stuffed dead animals, paintings, and wax figures. People paid to see them because they were the educational and scientific exhibits of the day. No one could explain why a baby could be born with a missing arm or leg, or why a person might appear to be completely white, or albino. Siamese, or conjoined, twins fascinated the public, too. Scientists lectured about the people on exhibit. Music, dancers, and short skits were added to the exhibit lecture program, and audiences stayed in their seats longer (and paid more for their tickets).

In the 1840s Phineas T. Barnum (P. T. Barnum) opened the American Museum in New York City. It was a museum and entertainment center, where families brought a picnic lunch and spent the day wandering through the exhibits and watching the variety acts. It was very popular, entertaining 41 million visitors before it burned down in 1868.

After the fire, P. T. Barnum closed the museum and turned his attention to his circus, making it a huge success. Others quickly copied the American Museum on a smaller scale, launching the era of "dime museums" in cities and small towns across America.

Every city had at least one dime museum; New York City had more than 50. The human curiosities were still the main attraction, and the term "freak show" became a popular term for them. Unusual-looking people were in high demand for the freak shows and would travel from town to town, appearing for a few weeks until everyone who might pay admission to see them had done so; then they moved on to the next scheduled town. Traveling circuses were popular, too, and the dime museums competed with them for human curiosities. There weren't enough exotic or unusual-looking people to fill the demand for freaks, so frauds often pretended or faked unusual features to lure paying audiences.

Frauds might pretend to be conjoined (or Siamese) twins, joined from birth at the hip, while they were really just bound together under their clothing. It was common for a "wild man" to appear, unshaven and acting like an animal, while being held in a cage. Strong men also joined freak shows, as well as very skinny ones (the Human Skeleton), and anyone with a physical attribute they could exaggerate, such as the Fat Woman (who even wore padded clothing) or the Bearded Lady (usually a man wearing a dress).

Novelty acts, magicians, exotic people from far-off lands and self-made freaks filled the sideshow platform at circuses and dime museums. Eventually, audiences lost interest in dime museums as circuses and vaudeville shows took their place. By the time World War I began, dime museums had faded away in cities, with a few remaining in country towns.

from other magicians as well as creating his own. He also sold some of his tricks, and published books telling how an illusion was done to keep others from trying to copy him.

The first illusion Harry bought was called the Substitution Trunk trick, sometimes also called Metamorphosis. Metamorphosis is the process of changing from one form to another, such as when a caterpillar turns into a butterfly or a tadpole becomes a frog. In Metamorphosis, Harry would make Jack "disappear" onstage behind a screen, reappearing on the other side of the screen as if by miracle.

Harry and Jack performed Metamorphosis until the two decided to split up. Harry then invited his brother Dash to do the act with him, and Dash and Harry

Coney Island was a beachfront amusement park. Houdini worked there in a tent with a strongman act.

17

1893 Columbian Exposition.

Plaisance, a street outside the fair that was packed with sideshows, booths, vendors, and amusements.

Working in a dime museum outside the actual fair grounds was not the same as appearing "in" the fair, but to the Houdini Brothers, it was a major step up. They did 20 shows a day for $12 a week. They did sleight of hand, rope tricks, and card tricks. Harry even performed as a yogi. Wearing dark makeup and a loose white robe, he chanted and played a lyre to conjure seeds into sprouting small plants, then revealed three-foot-high mango trees, right before the audience's eyes. He pretended to be a Hindu conjurer, doing tricks with snakes in baskets as well as the "growing plant" trick.

It was about this time that Harry came up with his handcuff escape act. He called himself Harry Houdini, Handcuff King and Escape Artist. It didn't seem to get much attention in the beginning.

The Houdini Brothers performed at the fair for about a month. Then Dash went home to New York, and Harry got a job at a dime museum in Chicago. It was the lowest rung of the entertainment ladder, but he was never too proud to take a booking. He did card tricks and simple conjuring tricks.

became the new Houdini Brothers. Harry learned that a huge world's fair was opening in Chicago and got them into a show on the Midway at the 1892 World's Columbian Exposition. The fair was a great opportunity for a performer to gain attention from a large audience from all over the country and even the world. But the Houdini Brothers weren't exactly performing in the fair itself. They worked at one of the dime museums on the Midway

Here he learned a valuable lesson about show business, that showmanship was as essential as talent. He knew a performer, Mattie Lee Price, who wowed audiences by demonstrating some very simple laws of gravity. She was one of several women who demonstrated mysterious physical abilities. Some used electrical charges—very new and not understood by the public—to lift articles. These petite women used the laws of physics, particularly those involving movement, to pit their strength against several strong men onstage.

ELECTRIC GIRLS

"Electric girls" appeared on stages across the country during the late 1800s. Electricity was still a mysterious force, often misunderstood. Spiritualism, or the belief that spirits from another world communicated to unique individuals through some unexplainable force, was very popular. Several young women, most from the state of Georgia, began performing feats of strength, which they attributed to unseen—usually unknown—forces.

The Victorian era of the 19th century was rapidly coming to a close when the electric girls began performing. Earlier

The Midway section of the world's fair, where the Houdini Brothers performed. The Ferris wheel is in the distance and a hot air balloon floats above some of the sideshow booths.
LIBRARY OF CONGRESS LC-USZ62-51866

in the century, women never appeared onstage; it was viewed as unladylike. In plays, male actors usually portrayed female characters. By the 1880s, however, that was changing a bit—at least for the electric girls, who found an unusual way to gain access to the performance stage. At the time, female Spiritualists were welcomed as speakers. They would pretend

19

Annie Abbott, the Little Georgia Magnet, defied strong men to lift her.

PANORAMA OF MAGIC, DOVER PUBLICATIONS, 1962

to interpret messages from another spirit world to curious audiences. Being a Spiritualist gave women a chance to enjoy power, attention, and income.

The most famous of these "female Sampsons," as Houdini called them, was Lulu Hurst, known theatrically as the Electric Girl or the Georgia Wonder. Lulu actually copied her act after a French woman, Angelique Cottin, who wowed Paris in 1846 with her ability to release energy that could send objects darting away from her, could prevent strong men from lifting a chair she sat on, and could lift a 60-pound table completely off the floor when she touched it with her apron. She claimed her abilities came from her spiritual powers.

In 1883 Lulu Hurst, only 14 years old, became the first American electric girl and wowed audiences by her unusual ability to overpower strong men and make canes, umbrellas, and chairs move simply at her touch. People said she was an amazing Spiritualist or "electrician," with supernatural powers. Hurst exploited her abilities and audiences' interest by performing across the country, traveling 20,000 miles by train in only two years. Financially secure, she retired quietly and others took her place.

Dixie Haygood, another Georgia woman, saw one of Hurst's performances and quickly followed in her footsteps, adding additional effects to the performance. She made a greater splash—doing big shows in England, Europe, Russia, and across the United States, using the stage name Annie Abbott, the Little Georgia Magnet.

Magicians, however, performed nearly the same feats onstage as the Spiritualists: making furniture rise in the air or making voices or objects appear. They resented the Spiritualists, because magicians didn't like people to think special tricks or effects were due to supernatural powers. Magicians wanted audiences to recognize that illusions were the result of practice and skill. They wanted audiences to recognize—and admire—their skill, not think it was something they didn't work hard to develop. So they began revealing how Spiritualists created their illusions.

Beginning in the middle 1800s, about the time the electric girls began appearing, magicians began using electrical devices in their acts. Robert-Houdin created a popular trick that used an empty metal box onstage. Anyone could lift it, of course, and volunteers from the audience came up and did so. Then, after a command from Robert-Houdin, the box would be stuck to the floor so solidly that the strongest volunteer couldn't budge it. The trick relied on an electromagnet hidden beneath the floor of the stage. When Robert-Houdin stepped on a hidden button on the floor, the electric current flowed to create the magnet, holding the box in place. When he stepped off the button, the electrical connection was disconnected.

While none of the electric girls ever told how they did some of their tricks, several appear to have been done the same way. With metal plates in her shoes, Dixie Haygood (Annie Abbott) would have been impossible to lift. She also used a young child, her son, to do a similar trick. When she held his hand and looked into his eyes, men were unable to lift him off the floor of the stage.

By combining the mysteries of electricity and Spiritualism, young women traveled across the country, performing feats of physical strength onstage before huge audiences. The mysterious subjects as well as the growing attitude toward women's rights created the opportunity. Dixie Haygood's son later wrote that after his father was shot and killed during an argument, his mother was left with three children (one a newborn) and had to do something to make ends meet. "There was nothing for mother to do but go on the stage," he said.

Scientists and physicians studied the electric girls, examining their bodies and watching their acts. None could figure out how they were able to do such feats. "Little Lulu" Hurst was invited to Alexander Graham Bell's laboratory in Washington, D.C., where she performed her feats while scientists and observers from the Smithsonian Institution watched. She lifted a 200-pound man off the floor while perched on a pair of weight scales. The viewers were puzzled because when she lifted the man up, only his weight registered on the scales.

Lulu herself later admitted there were no tricks to her performance, claiming it was based only on "unrecognized mechanical principles." Dixie Haygood, however, went beyond simple physics demonstrations, apparently using electricity and magnets in some manner. Such acts were popular and easy ways for women to earn money—Lulu received licensing payments for her name's use on soap and cigars. Farm equipment was sold for years with the advertised claim, "As strong as Lulu Hurst."

Houdini knew that Lulu Hurst had used the principle of a lever and fulcrum to fool audiences into thinking she had some supernatural power. He met one of the more successful electric girls while performing in dime museums in Chicago after the fair. There he watched as Mattie Lee Price presented a strength act like Hurst's, but promoted it as a scientific study. Her husband, Mr. White, was her assistant, and Houdini thought he was the main reason for her success.

What impressed Houdini most was how important Mattie Lee's husband was, because of the way he introduced her and how he kept the audience's attention and admiration during the act. It was her husband, as emcee, who made the act interesting and exciting for the audience.

Houdini remarked, "For a time she was a sensation of the highest order, for which thanks were largely due to the management of her husband, a wonderful lecturer and a thorough showman." But Mattie Lee took up with another man and left her husband. Her new husband was not nearly as talented at winding up the audience during her shows. Without Mr. White and his skill at selling the act, Houdini said she "sank out of sight."

Lift a Person with One Hand

This trick seems to really be a trick on the audience. You'll be lifting a person up into the air, but not in the way you might think. They will rise because the chair rises.

You'll need a straight-back solid dining chair. Ask a volunteer to sit in the chair, then tell them you will lift them and the chair into the air using only one hand. To do so, you'll use the concept of a lever and fulcrum to move a mass of weight.

You'll stand behind the chair and pull it backward and down with your hand. That will raise the seated person up into the air. The trick is that you don't really lift the entire chair off the ground, only two legs of the chair. The person's feet will be lifted off the ground, however, and as he or she edges back farther toward the back of the chair, they are pushing the load closer to the fulcrum—just what you want! The lever is the chair, the fulcrum is where the chair leg touches the floor, and the load, of course, is the volunteer!

When performing onstage, electric girls would ask several people to sit on top of one another's laps on the chair at once, lifting them all together on the same principle.

You can see from the drawing how a lever, such as a board, can lift up a load if a fulcrum lies between the place where you apply the effort and the load. In the drawing, the board is resting on the fulcrum. Muscular effort alone couldn't lift up the weight, but when a lever—which is considered a simple machine—is used, it concentrates the effort or force and makes it possible to move the load.

The spot on the lever where the load rests makes a big difference in how much effort it takes to press down the lever in order to lift the load. If the fulcrum is midway between the load and the muscle effort, there isn't any advantage to using a lever—it takes as much muscle to lift the load as to simply lift it directly without a lever. When the load is placed at one end, however and the fulcrum moved closer to the load, making the effort section farther from the fulcrum, it takes a lot less effort or strength to lift the load. At this point, you have "mechanical advantage."

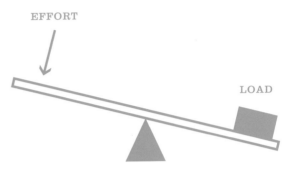

Here's how a first-class lever works. The board is the lever, because by pushing down with effort on one end, the fulcrum helps lift the load that sits on the other end of the board.

Show off your "strength" by using a chair as a fulcrum to lift someone.

23

Houdini said, "this was one of the most positive demonstrations I have ever seen of the fact that showmanship is the largest factor in putting an act over." He realized that Mattie Lee Price "was a marvelous performer," but "without her husband-lecturer she was no longer a drawing card, and dropped to the level of an ordinary entertainer even lower, for her act was no longer even entertaining."

Later, Houdini would advise young performers about the importance of showmanship, counseling them to arrange their acts by beginning with something simple, then moving to more difficult and impressive illusions, and closing with something "showy and apparently difficult." Houdini said it was OK to perform simple tricks others had done for years. "Don't lose confidence in an effect because it has been presented many times before. An old trick in *good hands* is always new. Just see to it that yours are *good hands*." He kept trying new tricks, too. "Don't allow yourself to 'go stale' in your act," he advised. "Keep up your enthusiasm! There is nothing more contagious than exuberant enthusiasm, and it is sure to 'get' an audience."

Here's how the *New York Times* newspaper described Lulu's show in July, 1884:

CHILDREN IN HER HANDS

**Twenty club athletes retire discomfited
Lulu Hurst moves them around at will**

Twenty strong well-built club athletes, many of them rubber-shod, with short coats buttoned close around their shapely chests, climbed on to the stage at Wallack's Theater last night and labored like blacksmiths for an hour to either tire out or "expose" Lulu Hurst, "the phenomenon of the nineteenth century," as the billboards call her. About 300 less muscular but equally enthusiastic club men gathered in the front seats to watch the fun. The athletes retired from the stage after the performance covered with perspiration and confusion. The Georgia girl, who had tossed them about like so many jackstraws, was perfectly cool and not in the least tired. She professed to feel in better condition and capable of greater demonstration at the close of the performance than at the beginning of it.

A man weighing nearly 200 pounds dropped into the chair and the phenomenon lifted him as though he were a boy of 10 years. The audience grew interested and fully 60 people pushed their way onstage and kept their eyes on the girl's hands and legs.

Four Against One

This was another of the strong women's acts, which are called "resistance acts" because they are designed so a smaller person can resist the strength and force of others much stronger.

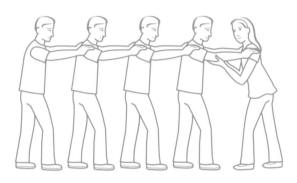

If you push up beneath the challenger's elbows, you weaken the force against your shoulders.

To perform this trick, you'll need several kids—four makes an effective presentation. You stand facing the smallest of the four challengers, who rests his or her hands on your shoulders. Then each challenger, from smallest to largest in size, stands behind one another with hands on one another's shoulders.

Next, bend your elbows, and place your hands under the first challenger's elbows, placing one of your feet in front of the other, knees slightly bent. As the first challenger in line begins to push against your shoulders, the others in line push on one another's shoulders to push the line forward. You can deflect their force by pushing the first one's elbows upward.

When you push up against the first challenger's elbows, you redirect his or her force against you up and away. The pushing from the rest of the challengers doesn't make any difference, because their force is stopped by the principle of inertia. None of them can exert more force than his or her own. Each person's body absorbs the pressure from the person behind him or her.

Little Lulu used a variation of this trick in her New York City act. The girl faces away from the line of men with her arms outstretched, bracing her hands against the wall. No matter how much the entire line of men pushes against her, she can't be pressed against the wall. In Lulu's act, the line of sweating men collapsed on the floor, and a newspaper story later described her as only using the "tips of her fingers" to support herself against the wall.

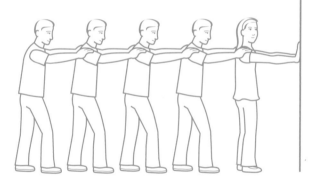

By bracing herself against the wall with her hands and keeping her arms straight, the girl can deflect the force of the man pushing against her back.

> ## "Walk right out on the stage and tell your tale to your audience, and perhaps many will believe it."
>
> —HOUDINI

When it was over, Major J. B. Pond, a lecture manager and promoter, told the reporter, "I have made a study of odic power. She can, I think, be trained to exert her will on inanimate objects. She could open a door by simply willing it."

Talk like that kept the audiences coming, even though many who attended such shows realized it was all based on simple laws of gravity and force, concepts studied today in school physics lessons.

MYSTERIOUS HARRY AND LA PETITE BESSIE

After the 1893 Exposition, Harry and Dash got back together and toured again, performing as the Houdini Brothers in a wide range of places, including Coney Island. It was about this time Wilhelmina Beatrice Rahner entered 20-year-old Harry's life. Bess, as she was known, was part of a song and dance act called the Floral Sisters. She was 18 years old and had joined the act after working as a seamstress for a traveling circus. Bess was very tiny and looked far younger than she was.

The Houdini Brothers and the Floral Sisters were performing at the same

hall, and Dash made a date with the girls to meet on the beach. Harry and Bess hit if off immediately—it was love at first sight. Three weeks later they announced they were married. Bess worried about breaking the news to her mother, especially because her new husband was a poorly paid Jewish magician. The Rahner family was strictly Catholic, in an era when people seldom married across religious lines. Mrs. Rahner was upset about the marriage and wouldn't acknowledge or visit them. (Twelve years later, when Bess was seriously ill, Harry would beg Mrs. Rahner to visit her daughter. She agreed, Bess recovered, and the ice was broken. From that point, she adored her son-in-law and stayed on good terms with Bess.)

Harry, too, worried about how his mother would accept his sudden marriage. He figured she wouldn't accept Bess because she was Catholic. Mrs. Weiss, however, was thrilled to bring Bess into the family—after all, the Weisses had six sons and only one daughter. Bess and Harry moved into the crowded boardinghouse rooms with the Weiss family. For the first few nights, Bess slept with some neighbors who had an extra bed in their room.

Balls or Coins Trick

ere's a clever way to use the same principle of inertia as in the resistance acts. It was explained in *Scientific American* magazine in the 1800s.

You can use billiard balls, marbles, or coins. All must be the same size and weight. Line up about six of whatever item you chose, all touching sides. Tell the audience you will remove one without touching any in the group.

Taking another ball, marble, or coin, roll or slide it to hit against the end of the row. That will jar one loose at the other end. You have removed one without touching the row. It will work for two, three, or any number you choose, because the law of inertia and momentum means that each ball passes along the same amount of force it receives, and no more.

You may have to practice a few times, but the effect is simply magical. The balls that remain still show inertia. Those that move show momentum.

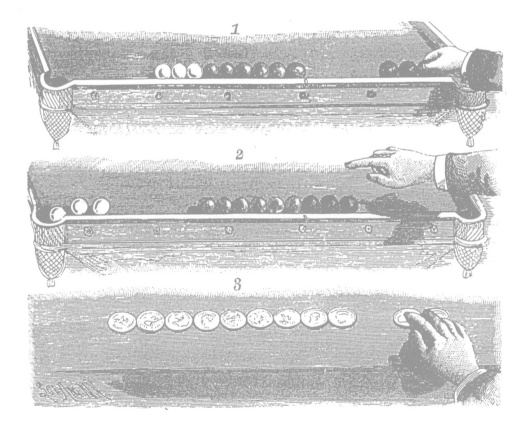

Balls or Coins Trick.
MAGIC, ARNO PRESS, 1977 (REPRINT OF 1897 EDITION)

"Never tell an audience how good you are, they will soon find that out for themselves." —HOUDINI

The RANNEYS · Americas Greatest comedy Act.

1st YEAR MARRIED Life.

1st Professional PICTURE 1894

Bess and Harry, during the first year they were married.

Bess replaced Dash in the Houdini Brothers act. One advantage was her petite size, which made it much easier for her to hide inside various boxes, trunks, and other equipment onstage. After the brothers' last performance together, Harry made both Bess and Dash swear a promise to him. He took them to a dark, lonely bridge on a cloudy night. At midnight he took their hands and said, "Beatrice, Dash, raise your hands to heaven and swear you will both be true to me. Never betray me in any way, so help you God." Dash and Bess repeated the vow. Harry kissed Bess and shook hands with Dash, saying, "I know you will keep that sacred oath."

Harry and Bess, now The Houdinis, worked hard, performing at every opportunity. They worked for several years in dime museums, doing the same act nine times a day, for $18 a week. In the 1920s, when they were successful, they would do the same act twice a day for $1,800 a week, ten times that amount. At the peak of his career, Houdini would make several hundred thousand dollars on a single tour. But starting out, it was very slow going.

Their first act included the Needle Trick and Metamorphosis (the Substitution Trunk). Harry learned how to do the Needle Trick from another performer he had worked with in a freak show. To do it, he placed a handful of needles and a length of thread in his mouth, appeared to chew and swallow them, then opened his mouth and brought out the needles, threaded. Harry and Bess were great at Metamorphosis. Harry continued to do the Needle Trick now and then, but Metamorphosis became their most famous and longest-running act. In this trick, Bess got into a large wooden box onstage, Harry closed the lid, and minutes later she stepped out from behind a curtain as he rose up out of the box. Audiences loved it and the couple continued performing it for years.

The Houdinis were happy. They loved each other deeply and enjoyed working on the magic act together. They traveled a lot, doing shows in strange towns and catching the train to the next. They did not have any children but seemed to wish they had some. Harry invented a pretend son he named after his father. He would write letters to Bess, passing them via the maid, telling her how the "boy" was doing in school and about his adventures growing up. Eventually Harry quit writing the letters about the pretend son, when the boy was elected president of the United States. At one time, Bess told a friend she

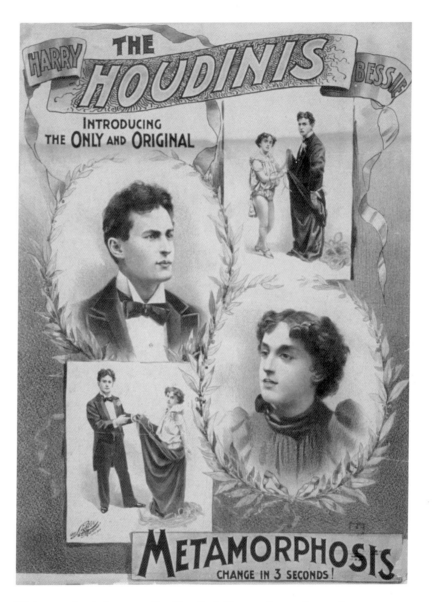

Metamorphosis became the Houdinis' longest-running act.

Harry Houdini could make even simple card tricks seem sensational.

was sewing clothing for her pretend daughter, who would wed soon.

Dogs seemed to take the place of children in the Houdinis' lives. They had a succession of dogs that went everywhere with them. They packed a dog pillow in their trunk and took them along as they did shows across the country and in Europe. They were given their beloved Charlie in Europe, and later, another dog would take his place: Bobby, the Handcuff Escape Dog. The Houdinis never did have a child of their own.

The Houdinis performed as a working act in dime museums, entertaining the audience until the main attraction, the freaks, appeared. Freaks were unusual people who would come out and stand on the stage as the master of ceremonies told their story. The story, which may or may not have been true, is what kept the audience interested. Freaks didn't actually perform, they just exhibited themselves to curious customers. Harry and Bess became good friends with many of these people. Years later he explained that "I often sat at the table with Unthan the Legless Wonder, who would pass me the sugar, and the fat lady, Big Alice, would obligingly sit at the edge of the table so as to give poor little Emma Shaller, the Ossified

Girl, plenty of room. Jonathan Bass, who was announced as his own living headstone, did not become the cemetery ornament he threatened to be. Blue Eagle, the man who broke boards over his head to show the solidity of his cranium, is running an embroidery shop in New Jersey. Mexican Billy Wells, who had cobblestones broken on his head, is soliciting for a photograph gallery."

Houdini gained more than friendship from working with the freak shows. They taught him how to promote his abilities, and even several of the tricks or techniques he later would use in his acts. He quickly learned to promote his act with posters and flyers. The Houdinis began calling themselves Monsieur and Mademoiselle Houdini or Mysterious Harry and La Petite Bessie. Sometimes they were simply The Great Houdinis. But it didn't seem to matter how hard they worked (20 shows a day at Huber's Dime Museum) or how frugally they lived, their future seemed to be going nowhere. At one point, Bess became discouraged and left the act, leaving Harry to finish up their contract performing solo.

As Harry liked to joke, they were "two young people, trying to make an honest million."

CREATING TALENT

People who performed in freak shows and sideshows were usually very creative people who used whatever talents they had to make a living by getting attention. Today many of these sorts of people are listed in the *Guinness Book of Records* or in *Ripley's Believe It or Not*. In the late 1800s and early 1900s, they worked for dime museums and circuses. Like other performers who developed an unusual talent or skill, the Houdinis surprised and puzzled their audience by using their bodies in unusual ways. They used escape tricks and magic to mystify their audience, like many other entertainers of the day.

Barnum & Bailey's freak show included Tattooed People, a Bearded Lady, Wild Men of Borneo, a Moss Haired Girl, a Sword Swallower, the Orissa Twins (joined by their clothing!), and Skeleton Dude.

A freak show audience at a Vermont fair.

Becoming the Handcuff King

In 1896, after Harry and Bess had been performing together for about a year, Harry arranged an interview with the Welsh Brothers Traveling Circus, which made Bess feel more hopeful about their future in show business. Together they lugged their trunk full of props and belongings to the muddy field where the circus was camped. It was raining and dark—and this was their last hope to move up from dime museums into a real circus. The gig would last at least six months, which would give them some security and income.

When they met Mike Welsh, one of the owners, he asked them, "Well, what do you do?"

Harry answered, "Anything."

A CIRCUS EDUCATION

Welsh assigned Harry to work in the Punch and Judy puppet show, and Bess to do mind reading. Harry would do magic acts, Bess would sing and dance, and they'd do the Metamorphosis trunk trick. They would also walk in the circus parade each day, drumming up interest around town for the afternoon show.

Together they would earn $25 a week and meals. For living arrangements they got a sleeping cot in the circus train car, which was partitioned with cardboard dividers and curtains. After agreeing to the conditions and the job, Bess collapsed on their cot in disappointed tears. Never giving up, Harry grabbed a notepad and began writing songs for Bess to sing for her act.

A few nights later Harry discovered he was expected to pitch in even more. When Projea, the Wild Man of Mexico, became too ill to go on and the crowd began yelling for his appearance, Houdini was appointed to take his place. The manager told him, "Put some paint on your face and get in the cage. They want the wild man." Houdini messed his hair and painted red streaks on his cheeks, blue on his chin, and black rings around his eyes. He tore up a burlap sack to create a caveman outfit and got in the cage. He would be Projea. Stagehands pushed the cage onto the stage and the stage manager pushed raw meat into the cage as the audience jeered. Houdini got into the act, tearing the meat with his teeth, growling, and grabbing and shaking the bars now and then. People cheered and several threw cigarettes and coins into the cage. Later Harry divided up the cigarettes with the rest of the cast, as he never smoked.

Houdini was a willing worker, doing whatever it took to learn the ropes and respecting his coworkers, who helped him a lot. One freak, an armless man, taught him to use his toes as fingers, a skill Harry practiced until he would later be able to untie ropes and use keys in handcuffs with his toes. He learned how to do sword swallowing, fire eating, and the strongmen techniques. He learned from a Japanese acrobat how to seem to swallow objects and regurgitate them at will by hiding them in his throat. All these odd skills seemed useless to others, but

Houdini would use them all later on when he needed to hide keys to locks and other devices for his escape acts.

Harry was always ambitious, and while working for the circus he also sold soap and grooming supplies to the other performers. Bess earned two dollars extra by singing songs from the official circus songbook that was for sale. They didn't have many expenses, so they mailed $12

The Houdinis are in the front row in this photograph of the Welsh Brothers Traveling Circus.

PHINEAS T. BARNUM (1810—1891)

Known also as P. T. Barnum, Phineas T. Barnum was a showman who organized and promoted low-cost entertainment to the widest audience.

Phineas began earning money by exhibiting an elderly blind woman. She was a former slave named Joyce Heth. Phineas told everyone she had been George Washington's nurse and was over 160 years old. Joyce was only 80 when she died, so they weren't telling the truth to audiences. But Barnum had discovered how to make his fortune. He bought a small dime museum in New York City and

FAMOUS AMERICANS,
DOVER PUBLICATIONS, 2005

expanded it to create the American Museum. It held dozens of fascinating exhibits, both animal and human. He also created a few hoaxes, knowing people enjoyed being puzzled about things, especially if the spectacles were heavily advertised and promoted.

The American Museum burned in 1865, moved to a new location, and burned down again in 1868. After that, Barnum went into the circus business. He was already in his sixties at that time, but he put together P. T. Barnum's Grand Traveling Museum, Menagerie, Caravan, and Hippodrome. It became simply The Greatest Show on Earth, and later, after joining with James Bailey, the Barnum and Bailey Circus. He was the first to purchase his own circus train, making traveling easier for the whole show. Barnum pioneered the traveling circus, the first to truly "take the show on the road."

each week to Harry's mother. Harry always tried to keep his word to his dying father to take care of her.

When the circus season ended, the Houdinis worked for a vaudeville show touring New England. Harry played the part of Professor Morat, a European hypnotist. He "hypnotized" audience members and exhibited how he could endure pain without feeling it. Audience members would poke him with pins and needles while he was in a hypnotic trance. He'd learned the techniques for enduring pain from one of the circus performers who stuck pins into her body. The show fizzled out, however, and the Houdinis were soon back looking for work.

EXCELLENT ESCAPES

Harry and Bess soon signed on with Marco the Magician, who was touring the Maritime Provinces in Canada. The Metamorphosis act went over very well, but by July the show went bust. Harry had begun doing escape stunts, trying to move beyond simple magic acts. He began doing handcuff escapes as part of Metamorphosis. Then he bought a set of theatrical handcuffs and an escape act from a magic dealer in Boston. Now Houdini began doing Metamorphosis while

Dissolving Rings Trick

his is a traditional ring trick. It needs a bit of practice before a performance, but is well worth it.

MATERIALS

Piece of cord about 4 feet long

6 rings about 3 inches across
(Rings from curtain rods or shower curtains are perfect)

Handkerchief or scarf

Tie one ring to the middle of the length of cord, as shown, by looping the cord through the ring and then passing the two ends through the loop and pulling tight (A). Show the audience that it is firmly secured. String the cords through the center of the rest of the rings so they rest on top of the first ring (B). Ask two audience members to hold the ends of the cord. Announce that you will magically take the rings off the cord while the volunteers continue holding the ends of the cord.

Drape the scarf over the rings, announce your special phrase—"Abracadabra!" or something similar—and command the rings to drop off the cord. As you reach up under the scarf, the rings fall into your hand.

Here's how it works: As you reach up under the scarf, pull the loop in the cord down and around the first ring (C). That will unfasten it; it will drop, and so will all the rest. The secret is in the fact that the first ring was fastened with a loop that can be pulled apart—not a knot as it appeared.

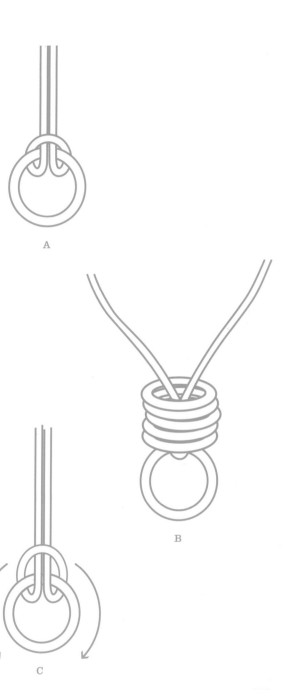

Harry bound by chains and handcuffs.

handcuffed. He began asking for anyone in the audience to lend him handcuffs for the act, just as he had been asking for a volunteer's jacket for Metamorphosis. It was impressive when he donned a borrowed jacket, and as the trick unfolded, Bess appeared on the other side of the screen wearing the same jacket. Handcuffs added complexity to the act.

While lots of audience members might have a jacket to lend, no one carried handcuffs around with them. That's when Harry decided he would borrow them from the right source: the police.

In 1895, while performing in Gloucester, Massachusetts, Harry went to the police station and offered to escape from any handcuffs they could put on him. They went along with him, and he escaped from two types they used. Harry made sure the newspaper carried a story about the whole thing, and he began repeating the police challenge—always with newspaper coverage—in every town he performed in.

But the audience couldn't be there to see it, and he couldn't bring the police to the show. Or could he? In New Brunswick, the local police met his challenge, arriving at the show with cuffs in hand for him to try to escape. They even brought heavy chains and leg irons onto the stage. After they wrapped chains around his body, they handcuffed his hands behind his back and locked the shackles on his feet. They helped him into the small cabinet he used for the act, then pulled the curtain to hide him inside it. In only a few minutes, he popped out, loose chains and handcuffs in his hand. The audience went wild— many believing it possible only because Houdini was somehow supernatural.

Harry decided that escaping from dramatic situations might be his calling— at least it guaranteed publicity to pack in the crowds at his evening shows. He arranged to make a dramatic escape no one had done before: he would escape from rope ties while tied to the back of a horse. He arranged for a local stable to supply a horse and the town newspaper's reporters to show up. The crowd assembled, eager to see the young stranger free himself. Harry mounted the horse, had his hands bound behind his back, and had his feet tied together with ropes under the horse's belly. Then things went terribly wrong. Something spooked the horse and it began bucking, then it took off running, and Harry couldn't stop it. The trick went out of control. Harry couldn't be bucked off the animal—he couldn't even escape the ties because the horse was galloping wildly. A few miles down the road, the horse tired and Harry was able to work himself free from the ropes. He'd finally completed the escape, but the audience wasn't able to see it. He learned to plan ahead for every possibility and to practice every act beforehand.

Harry's next escape act would avoid animals and put him entirely in control of the props. He decided to escape the confines of a straitjacket, a specially designed jacket used to control violent people. Hospitals and police departments used them to subdue people who might hurt themselves or others. The jacket had long sleeves with the ends sewn closed to encase the arms and hands. The ends of the sleeves had bands that buckled to the back of the jacket. Once placed on a person with their arms crisscrossed in front and the sleeves fastened behind, there was no way a person could pull it off or wriggle out of it. Until Houdini. He added a straitjacket escape to his act, slipping out of it while hidden inside his stage cabinet. Audiences didn't think much of it.

When the show ended, the Houdinis began looking for work again. Harry called himself Cardo, the King of Cards. He and Bess did a comedy routine.

Magic Knot Trick

This trick uses some of the same techniques Harry Houdini relied on: agility, flexibility, and clever thinking. He was famous for slipping his arms and wrists out of rope ties. He spent lots of time studying knots and knot tying and untying to perfect his act. Here's a trick he probably discovered early in his career.

This simple trick will impress anyone and will make you the center of attention as you challenge your friends.

MATERIALS

Piece of string, 2–3 feet long (A long shoelace is perfect)

Tabletop or desktop

Present the challenge: is it possible to tie a knot in a string without letting go of the ends?

Pass the string around and let a few people try it. They won't be able to do it. Show how easy it is by laying the string out across the table in front of you. Then, cross your arms as shown, tucking one hand behind and one in front of your opposite arms.

Pick up the ends of the string with your fingers and, while holding onto the string, pull the left hand to the left and the right hand to the right, unfolding your arms. A knot will automatically tie in the string.

The trick works because when you crossed your arms, you created the knot with your arms. Then, when you pulled the string, the knot moved from your arms to the string.

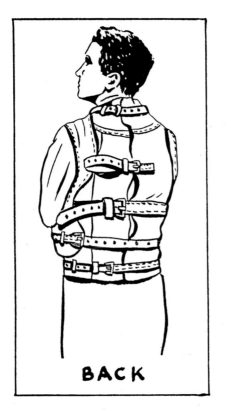

BACK   FRONT

Harry tried escaping
from a straitjacket.
HOUDINI ON MAGIC

Nothing seemed to work, and they had a hard time getting paid at the end of each engagement. Bess got sick, and Harry tried to open a magic school, intending to reveal all his secrets to make a quick income. He advertised it but had no takers except one student, an older gentleman from Chicago. He created a catalog of magic tricks called *Magic Made Easy*

and tried to sell his knowledge, but the orders barely trickled in.

They got a show booking in Milwaukee, but the manager swindled them out of their pay. They went on to Chicago where Harry tried gambling at card games to earn money for food. At one point things were so bad they lived for a week on two rabbits Harry purchased for a quarter. Down on their luck, Bess and Harry eagerly accepted a 15-week stint with Dr. Hill's California Concert Company. They would be selling tonics for an old-time traveling medicine show out West.

HINT OF DANGER

While traveling to join Dr. Hill's troupe, the Houdinis ran into a problem that almost ruined the opportunity for them. They needed to switch trains at 3:00 A.M., and their next train was leaving immediately. The problem was they had four heavy trunks full of their belongings and show props. A couple of passengers tried to help them pull the trunks from one train to another, but they were nearly stranded, two trunks in each train, and no way to finish the transfer before the next train pulled away. Desperate, Harry decided to use his body—throwing

TRAVELING MEDICINE SHOWS

Medicine shows have a long history beginning in Europe during the 1500s and 1600s. Small groups of performers would work for a doctor to gather a crowd in order to sell a medicine potion. Upon entering a town, the troupe would parade through the streets with musical instruments, then stop at a street corner where the doctor would stand up on a wagon and begin his lecture about the tonic. Eventually European shows became more about the entertainment than the medicine, and the performers began doing things like pantomime. The doctor's role became that of master of ceremonies, or ringmaster, to the show.

In America, however, the medicine show remained focused on the medicine. Tonics were wildly popular because medical care was so poor. Trained physicians were few and far between in rural areas, and they didn't really have any cures for ailments anyway. Before antibiotics were invented in the 1940s, there just wasn't much a physician could do when someone was ill. That meant people turned to "secret" and "miracle" cures, which promised easy solutions to health problems, didn't cost much, and usually contained a large amount of alcohol.

Marketers gave their tonics catchy names, such as Cholera Balm, King of Coughs, and Wizard Oil. Claiming that a tonic was a Native American cure was very popular, because people thought Native Americans knew secret herbal cures that Europeans hadn't discovered. Many traveling medicine shows had a pretend Native American dressed in feathers and skins, or sold tonics with Native American names. Wild West themes and costumes were also popular. The medicine-show doctors dressed to get attention, wearing their hair in long flowing locks (especially good if they were selling tonics to fight baldness). Western-style clothing, or boots and black frock coats and silk top hats made them dramatic and got attention from small-town crowds.

Remedies were never admitted to be ordinary concoctions, but always said to be from some exotic far-off place, or a secret recipe hundreds of years old. During the sales talk, *shills* would sometimes be in the audience, shouting out about how wonderful the medicine was and how it had cured them. Shills were either part of the troupe or paid to promote the tonic.

In 1906 President Theodore Roosevelt signed the Pure Food and Drug Act, which set limits on medicines. From that time, medicines had to be properly labeled and could not advertise results they couldn't prove.

himself onto the tracks in front of the train that they were trying to board. He gripped one rail with his fingers and clamped his feet on the other. He refused to budge until the conductor helped load the trunks. A crowd gathered; several railroad men tried pulling him up but nothing worked. Finally, one of the conductors shouted to him that his trunks were onboard. He leaped up, brushed off his clothes, and joined a nervous Bess, who had been sure that it wouldn't work.

Harry now realized that he was at "the turning point in [his] career." He could understand that dramatic action was the key to getting attention. "That was the first time I realized the public wanted drama. Give 'em a hint of danger, perhaps of death—and you'll have 'em packing in to see you!" From then on, he became more dramatic in his escape acts, toying with danger and even putting himself into life-and-death situations.

The Houdinis adapted quickly to Dr. Hill's show. Hill, not a doctor at all, was young and theatrical, wearing his hair long and flowing, with a dramatic beard and the ability to speak in ways to move the crowd. He praised his homemade medicine with velvety language. His partner, Dr. Pratt, was his sidekick, a quiet,

serious-looking, white-haired old gentleman. They trooped from town to town with Dr. Pratt's organ perched on a carriage. Stopping at a street corner, Dr. Pratt began playing melodious tunes on the organ while Harry slapped a tambourine and Bess broke into song. Once a crowd had gathered around, Dr. Pratt would speak about his miraculous medical tonic that could cure just about anything people suffered from. Harry went through the group collecting money while Bess passed out the bottles of medicine. They would announce their upcoming show that evening, urging the crowd to come see their act at the local town hall.

The act was getting more polished, and people enjoyed it. Harry was getting better at escaping from handcuffs—at least he was able to get the audience to find it more exciting. He also did some illusions, such as changing ordinary water into ink, and some card tricks. In every town, he tried to get a local newspaper to cover the act, learning to seek attention and publicity however he could.

Buster Keaton, who became a famous film star, was a toddler when his parents worked for Dr. Hill's California Concert Company with the Houdinis. The Keatons did an Irish comedy routine. Bess and

Harry enjoyed the little boy. Harry even gave Buster his nickname, calling him "quite a buster" one day. One night the hotel the troupe was staying in caught fire. Bess ran upstairs and rescued the boy, who was sleeping in his room, saving little Buster Keaton's life.

THE HOUDINIS GET PSYCHIC

After a few weeks Dr. Hill came to Harry with a problem. The crowds just weren't coming in as they should. Something had to be done to recharge the show and get more people interested. Dr. Hill told Harry that he heard other traveling shows were using spirit mediums, raking in the dough by doing séances. Séances were gatherings where people tried to communicate with spirits of the dead, doing such things as levitating (rising in the air) and telepathy (silent communication through the mind). People known as "spirit mediums" ran such gatherings. Spiritualists were very popular in the 19th century, when many people thought there might be a scientific explanation for a spirit world.

Dr. Hill figured a Sunday evening program that included a spirit medium was just what the show needed. Just as Harry had taken the job of the wild man in the dime circus, he accepted the job of spirit medium for the medicine show. Harry had read books about spirit mediums and had learned some of their tricks during his years in show business. He transformed himself into Professor Houdini, or the Great Houdini, and Bess became Mademoiselle Beatrice Houdini, the Celebrated Psycrometic Clairvoyant. Harry would do the speaking and showmanship part of the act, building the excitement and tension, while Bess sat covered by a sheet, waiting to make contact with the spirit world.

To prepare for the Sunday evening act, they would search for information the minute they entered a new town. By gathering newspaper obituaries to see who had recently died and visiting the cemetery, noting the headstone information on the newest graves, they could use local names, dates, and events to impress the townspeople. Standing around gathering gossip or listening while in the local store or hotel dining room, the Houdinis pieced together enough to make it seem they truly had some special ability.

In one Kansas show they got the audience in an uproar when Bess attempted to connect with the spirit of a recently murdered young woman. She pretended

> ## "Travel helps us a lot—it is education."
>
> —HOUDINI

to be in a trance, covered with a sheet, while Harry got louder and louder, demanding she reveal the name of the killer. Bess pretended to struggle with the spirit, eventually collapsing on the stage—Harry shouted for a doctor in the house, and the audience went wild—surrounding the sheriff and demanding he find the killer. It was a hugely successful evening for Dr. Hill's show and proved to the Houdinis how important showmanship could be. After all, Bess had never announced the killer's name at all—but the audience had been on the edge of their seat with excitement and anticipation.

Bess was a very unlikely spirit medium. In fact, with her religious upbringing, she feared anything related to the devil and refused to entertain any talk about spirits. Harry told her how everything was faked, from information he gleaned by reading a book, *The Revelations of a Spirit Medium*. He played a mind-reading trick on her, revealing the name of her dead father written on his arm when he rubbed stove ashes over his skin. She screamed—fearful he had some devilish power. When he laughed and told her how he had learned to do the trick from the book, she gave in. She even did a

few mindreading acts and sometimes used the name Madame Marco in their early years.

The secret behind the act was a code that Bess and Harry used to communicate with one another during the show. It was based on Harry's reading of Robert-Houdin's book years earlier. Robert-Houdin and his young son pioneered an act called Second Sight, which Robert-Houdin had seen performed by others as early as the 1780s. For a time in the 1840s, it was the most popular show in Paris. Many magicians in Europe used the act during the mid-1800s, and the Houdinis polished it to perfection for their act in the medicine shows of the 1890s.

To perform Second Sight, Robert-Houdin and his young son would take the stage together. He blindfolded the boy, then promised the audience that his son could identify whatever object an audience member would hand to his father.

The boy, unable to see the item, could supposedly figure it out with "special" powers. There was nothing really special at all, but audiences were mystified and impressed. Robert-Houdin and his son had created a pattern and a code. The pattern was based on a coded list of items the audience members might present.

For example:

gloves

purse

umbrella

watch

The code was how the father secretly helped the boy figure out which item in the series he needed to call out. The code words matched the objects from the list:

gloves = can

purse = will

umbrella = try

watch = now

The father and son would memorize the list of matching words. Then during the show, when the boy was blindfolded and unable to see or touch the object, he could easily tell his father what item the audience member had chosen. His father simply used the cue words to begin the sentence, such as "*Can* you tell us what I am holding?" The boy's response would be, "Gloves." If the father wanted the boy to identify a gentleman's watch, he would say, "*Now*, tell us what I am holding."

It was simple, it always worked, and the audiences were amazed.

The Houdinis were skilled at Second Sight, using it to create their spirit medium show. Bess and Harry created their

Mind Reading with Secret Code

Create a secret message code to use with a partner. You can do this for a variety of things, not just magic shows. No one will be able to figure out how it's done!

Match up a list of numbers, colors, or items with a list of words that can be used to start sentences. Then select the word that matches the number you want your partner to name.

Here's a sample list, used by the Houdinis:

Answer

Say

Now

Tell

Please

Speak

Quickly

Look

Be quick

Can

To help your partner think of the number you have in mind, start your question with the matching word. For example:

"*Can* you tell us . . ." for number ten

"*Say* the number now . . ." for number two

"*Answer* now . . ." for number one

Harry Houdini used many codes; he even used a secret code in his personal diary so Bess couldn't read it!

own code in order to do mind-reading acts to entertain the audience. Years later they would continue their codes in various ways, in ordinary life as well as during performances.

One of the Houdinis' codes is listed below. They used it to identify numbers. For example, Harry would have an audience member whisper his age to him, he'd write it on a large card and show it silently to the audience. Bess, usually blindfolded, or in a trance and beneath a sheet, would then use her special powers to read the man's mind and tell the audience his age. Bess had no special powers, of course—she would learn what number to announce when Harry asked coded questions:

"*Say*, do you know the number?"

"*Quickly*, now, how old is this gentleman?"

Say meant three and *quickly* stood for eight, so when Bess announced the man was 38 years old, the audience was thoroughly impressed.

The new Houdini act—the Spiritualist séance—drew crowds and provided traveling funds for Dr. Hill's show. When the season ended, the Houdinis did a few séance shows on their own, but they weren't satisfied. Harry felt they were making money by lying to people, which he couldn't accept. He realized the people coming to see their act believed it was true, and he just couldn't continue. He said, "When it was all over I saw and felt that the audience believed in me. They believed that my tricks were true communications from those dear dead." Lying to people who were grief stricken over deaths of loved ones was just too much for the Houdinis. "From that day to this I have never posed as a genuine medium . . . I was chagrined that I should ever have been guilty of such frivolity and for the first time realized that it bordered on crime."

That put them right back at the bottom, however. Their only gig was with a melodrama group whose performances were so bad that Harry took up a false name and tried to disguise himself, which included filling his cheeks with wads of paper, so no one would recognize him onstage. As soon as they could get back on again with the Welsh Brothers Traveling Circus, they jumped at the chance. They toured the entire summer, doing only escape acts and Metamorphosis. Audiences were enthusiastic, and the circus began using the Houdinis' act to close the show each evening.

FAME COMES KNOCKING

By 1899 Harry had a few bookings in the Midwest, but the future certainly didn't look bright. Now 25 years old, he considered getting a job working at a lock factory, where his knowledge about locks and keys might be useful and where a steady paycheck might support them. In Chicago, however, things began to turn around. He was scheduled for an evening show, and to drum up publicity he went to a downtown police station, offering to demonstrate his ability to escape locked handcuffs to the officers when they reported in for roll call to start the day. Two hundred people assembled to watch, including newspaper reporters, of course.

Making it even more of a challenge, Houdini was stripped and searched and his mouth sealed with plaster of paris so he couldn't hide a key anywhere on his body.

Harry was locked into cuffs, disappeared into his cabinet, and emerged with the still-locked cuffs dangling from his free hands. The police force was shocked. They tried other cuffs, ropes, and everything they could think of for another hour, but he continued to emerge from his cabinet completely free from restraint. The next morning, he pounced on the

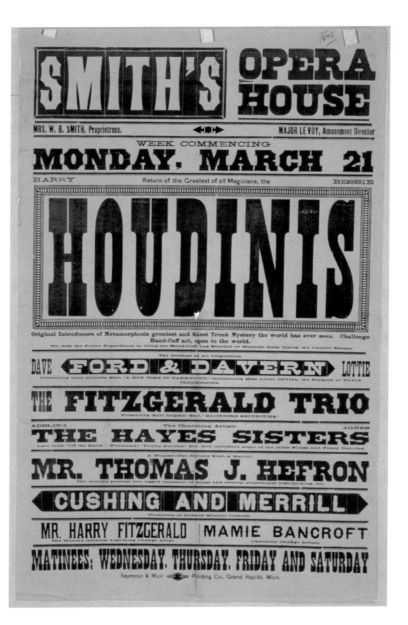

morning paper, running gleefully to Bess in the hotel room they were staying in. The Chicago newspaper carried the headline "Amazes the Detectives," along with a large drawing of Harry.

"I'm famous," he shouted. "Look at my picture in the papers!" He used the last cash they had to buy copies of the newspaper, then clipped out the story and mailed it to everyone he knew in show business.

Handcuff escape acts would be his claim to fame. For the rest of the week, police officers came by the Clark Street Museum in Chicago where Houdini was working with handcuffs for him to test. He'd offered to pay $100 to anyone who could bring a pair of cuffs he couldn't escape from. He welcomed the challenges during his evening show, where he put on the challenger's cuffs and retreated into his cabinet, where he unlocked or wriggled free from the cuffs out of sight.

All went well until one police officer, Sergeant Waldron, tried to trick him, popping a pair of altered cuffs on Houdini. He didn't realize they were plugged with a piece of metal inserted into each lock so it wouldn't move. After disappearing into the cabinet, the audience grew restless, and Waldron began shouting taunts at

him. After a full hour of struggle, Houdini emerged. He could only get one cuff off. The audience had gone; only Bess and Waldron remained. Bess was in tears. Houdini refused to give up, but he accused Waldron of rigging the cuffs. Waldron laughed and said, yes, he'd plugged the locks—no one could ever unlock them!

Houdini resorted to having the remaining cuff sawed off his wrist. He was furious. He knew his career, which was just getting off the ground, was over. Finished. Everyone had left the hall because he'd failed. The next morning he went in to the museum later than usual, figuring to retrieve his props and move on to the next town. Instead, the manager told him to get to work. No one seemed concerned that the trick had failed. In fact, the morning paper seemed to take Harry's side, with barely a mention of the failure. It read, "They were not practicable handcuffs at all, having no lock whatever. The affair was simply a joke on the part of the officer."

The house filled again that night, the trick went well, and the audience loved him. From that point on Houdini would do the same in every town he toured. He'd first meet the police officers at the station, exhibiting his ability to escape cuffs and other restraints. He would take along a newspaper reporter to chronicle the feat. The police chief usually appreciated Harry pointing out any weaknesses in their security practices at the station. The local paper would carry a big story, and that night the audience would roll in.

Houdini began helping police with other knowledge, too. He warned of tricks card sharks might use and warned against some of the ways hustlers cheated at card games.

Knowing how cheaters worked created a problem for Harry one night. He'd finished a show, it was late, and two men waited outside his dressing room door. They wanted him to break into a gambling house with them and fix some decks of cards so they could win big the next day. They offered to pay him $100—a very large sum in those days. Harry refused to help them and later recalled, "It's a dog eat dog world with gamblers, and the hundred looked good to me. But so did life—and I knew that if we got caught I'd be strung up for my pains. I declined with thanks."

But they wouldn't let him off that easy. When he was asleep back at his hotel room, someone rapped on his door telling him he had an urgent telegram to pick up down at the telegraph office. As he was hurrying in the dark to the office, he felt a cold gun barrel on his cheek. The men, armed now, made him go with them to the gambling house, where he got out his lock-picking tool and opened the back door. As soon as the lock was open, though, he jumped inside, pulling the door shut behind him and leaving the men outside. One of the men fired a shot at him through the wall. As he raised his hand to protect his face, the bullet lodged in his hand. It remained there the rest of his life.

At another Midwestern town, Harry helped out the local police without knowing it. Bess and Harry were working in St. Paul, Minnesota, and staying at a downtown hotel. Harry began to notice two suspicious men who appeared to be staying in the room directly across the hall. Every time Harry left or returned to the room, they opened their door and went out into the hallway. One afternoon he heard people fighting in the hallway and opened his door cautiously to check on the commotion. There were the two men, fighting with another man, who was wearing a long cape. As the two men pinned the other man to the floor, Harry saw he was bound with handcuffs.

VAUDEVILLE

Between 1890 and the 1930s, more than 4,000 magicians performed in vaudeville shows around the world. Vaudeville shows consisted of a series of short variety acts. Shows included acrobats, jugglers, comedians, singers, and trained animal acts. Twenty theaters in New York City alone featured acts, each running from eight minutes to an hour long in a total program lasting about two hours. Performers could spend two years traveling the United States and never appear in the same city twice. The soaring number of vaudeville shows created demand for acts that were fresh and different. Talented magicians could find plenty of opportunity.

Vaudeville made it possible for small-time entertainers to gain popularity and make money. The inexpensive novelty shows became the most popular form of entertainment in the United States by 1900. Ten-cent shows were affordable to everyone—just as the dime museums had been earlier.

In the heyday era of vaudeville shows, thousands of performers crisscrossed the country by train, doing shows at theaters scheduled by booking agents. The agents worked for two major circuits that controlled most of the vaudeville talent. The Orpheum Circuit ran the big theater chains in the West, and the Keith Circuit organized the East Coast. The industry was monopolized and controlled by the circuits. The circuits controlled all vaudeville acts, giving auditions and signing contracts for all performers. If any of the performers demanded too much salary, they could be cut off, unable to get any other theater bookings. But once performers signed on with a circuit, they could expect steady work, and if they were very popular the circuit would boost them as celebrities.

Traveling vaudeville performers might do 30 shows a week, moving quickly between small towns. Life on the road was hard, yet some performers took along their families, tucking children to bed in tiny backstage dressing rooms or in train car berths.

They were trying to rise from lives of poverty, and vaudeville was a way to make money using one's talent. One woman said, "Where else can people who don't know anything make so much money?" Some popular acts earned $1,500 a week—a huge amount in those days. The dream of hitting the big time kept performers plugging away in small towns for meager pay for years.

Vaudeville theaters tried to present clean family entertainment. They even censored performers' language, prohibiting the use of such words as *liar*, *devil*, *sucker*, *hell*, *spit*, *cockroach*, and others. In some theaters, women were paid to dress fashionably and sit in the audience, to bring in a better class of customers. Vaudeville was at the top of the show ladder. The circuit of theaters was a step above traveling circuses, and those were thought more highly of than the traveling medicine shows. When the Houdinis signed with the vaudeville show circuit, they had risen from the depths of show business. No more would they go back to doing dime museums or medicine shows. They hoped.

"We figured he'd come to you," one of the men told Harry. They were two local policemen who'd staked out Harry's room, guessing an escaped criminal they'd been tracking would probably come there to get Harry's help removing his handcuffs.

Harry and Bess moved on to an engagement in Omaha, Nebraska, where they were set to appear at their first really elegant theater. It was named the Creighton-Orpheum Theater, and it was like a palace. It had 800 velvet-upholstered seats, glittering chandeliers, and marble floors. The dressing rooms were sumptuous. It was a far cry from the traveling circus days.

The elegant theater enhanced his act, and Houdini did the finest escape performances ever. He continued his challenge to anyone who could produce cuffs he couldn't escape from. He became quicker, more polished, and seemingly unstoppable. His act became a hit, and the theater posters began claiming, "The Wizard of Shackles, A Man of Marvels." Eventually he hit on the name he liked best, The King of Handcuffs.

Martin Beck, head of the western Orpheum Circuit theater chain, saw Harry's act and signed him to perform the handcuff escape act and Metamorphosis. The Houdinis would get $60 a week, and a raise if they were successful.

And the Crowd Goes Wild!

Harry Houdini learned how to craft an international career from the simplest of things: wriggling out of handcuffs. Escape artists, as they called themselves, had been part of the traveling circus and dime museum world for several years. The fad started in Europe and spread to the United States as police departments became better organized and relied on restraints to control criminals. People liked to watch a guy—especially if he was small—get himself free from control by authority. In Europe, the beginning of the 20th century was a particularly harsh period for working people. Industrial jobs paid little, and landowners eager to increase agricultural production pushed many peasants off the land, replacing their labor with machines. Poor immigrants crowded the cities looking for work. Police and military control in Europe kept the public from rioting or overturning the governments. Anger flared up again and again for several years, and assassinations of public officials swept Europe and the United States. In the United States, President William McKinley was shot by an unemployed man and died a few weeks later after physicians failed to remove the bullet.

As Harry discovered, the public simply couldn't get enough of watching someone like himself—young and short in stature—escape and thwart police restraints.

HOW DID HE DO IT?

But what was Harry's secret? How did he do it? We can't tell for sure, because although he wrote several books and articles revealing how some magic tricks were performed, he didn't reveal many of his own special techniques. Lots of people tried to guess how he escaped locked cuffs. They thought he could shrink the size of his hand by dislocating the bones to create a smaller wrist that could slip through the locked cuff. Many simply accused him of having made a deal with the devil or said it was due to some supernatural ability to disintegrate and reappear, unfettered.

His secrets remained locked in a special trunk, Number 8, which he took everywhere. As his act became more successful, he traveled with more and more props and equipment to create the show, but Number 8 was handled only by Harry, Bess, or a trusted assistant. When he died, it went (locked) to his brother, Dash. When it was opened after Dash's death, the contents revealed little—it was packed full of a wide variety of tools: sewing needles, soldering supplies, keys, waxes, chalk, crayons, buttons and thread, pliers, calipers, drills, glass cutters, lock picks, screwdrivers, paintbrushes, wrenches, a candlestick, rulers, and measuring tapes. Lots of useful items, but nothing that revealed anything special.

Biographers today, such as Ruth Brandon, believe Houdini relied on one secret for the handcuff escape: keys. In his notes, a list of 28 handcuff models also tells which types of keys will open each. Harry even invented and patented a "split" key, which acted as a master key, that could open 95 percent of all British-made handcuffs. He also watched how the key was turned when the cuffs were locked on him—that would tell him which direction to work the inner lock with his pick or key.

Some handcuffs were so easy to unlock they could be popped by rapping them sharply against a hard surface. Harry wore a steel plate attached to his thigh, beneath his trousers. Inside the cabinet, he would rap the cuff hard against the plate. Many times he could pop the lock open with simple force.

Others figured he hid a special tool somewhere on his body—probably in his thick, curly, unruly hair. They were correct. Sometimes he did hide a lock pick there, just as he also hid one in the thick skin on the sole of his foot. Who would

Magic Key Trick

H ere's a clever trick using a padlock and your own "special" powers.

MATERIALS

Padlock

2 keys that will open the padlock

3 other keys

5 matching envelopes

Pencil

Bag, box, or hat

Prepare the act ahead of time with a gimmick, or trick, the audience doesn't see. Put one of the keys that will unlock the padlock into one of the envelopes, seal it, and make a small pencil dot on both sides of the envelope near one corner. That will mark it. Place it inside the bag.

Show the audience the padlock and four keys. Ask volunteers to try the keys in the padlock, figuring out that only one will open the lock. Have them put each

key in a separate envelope and seal it. Have them mix up the envelopes, then drop them into the bag. Pick out each envelope slowly and hold it up close to your head, as if your mind is reading what's inside, trying to locate the correct key. You'll be looking closely to find the envelope with the pencil mark.

If you have pulled out four envelopes and it still remains in the bag, say you must do it again, drop them all in, but position them separately from the last envelope in the bag. Then pull it out, be sure it has the mark, and declare your powers believe this to be the correct key. Tear open the envelope, hand it to a volunteer, and ask him or her to open the lock. Toss the envelope away yourself, so no one sees it was marked.

MARK

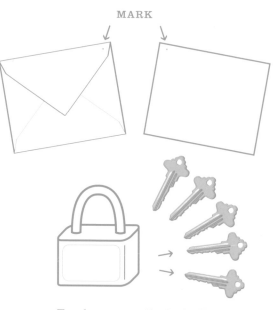

Two keys open the lock. Hide one in an envelope. Use the other to show how the lock opens.

find it there, even when searching him stripped naked?

CROSSING THE OCEAN

Houdini's escape act, Metamorphosis, and bookings with the Orpheum Theater circuit brought steady work and rising acclaim for him and Bess. They toured upscale theaters in San Francisco (even though their hotel room there was ridden with fleas!), Boston, Philadelphia, and Toronto. They grew accustomed to a frenetic pace and knew they had to push the act hard to become popular as quickly as possible in order to be a success in the competitive entertainment business.

Harry decided to book them on a tour of their own, and this time he shot for the moon. He wrote to a London company, asking for a booking. The manager refused, writing back, "I have no room for any addition to my company. I seldom change my artists." Houdini knew that he was now becoming so popular he could bring in the crowds if he had a chance. Or at least he thought he could. His posters held nothing back, claiming "Who created the biggest sensation in California since the Discovery of Gold in 1849? Why! Harry Houdini! The Only Recognized and Undisputed King of Handcuffs and Monarch of Leg Shackles." In the spring of 1900, he and Bess decided to take the chance. They bought tickets on a ship for London. They had no bookings in England, but Harry knew that problem would take care of itself.

London wasn't such a farfetched idea. Magicians had been doing very well there recently, and several old friends of Harry's kept in touch. He knew he could do as well as they had done if he had the chance.

On the trip, a huge problem surfaced that would plague Harry the rest of his days. No matter that he was in top physical shape, always an athlete in training, powerfully muscled, and able to excel at distance running and bicycling—Harry laid on the bed like a limp rag during most of the trip. He was incredibly seasick. Dizzy, vomiting, unable to stand or do much else, Harry suffered seasickness every time they traveled by boat. In that era, going by sea was the only way to travel to other continents—air travel would come later (and Harry would be in the thick of it when it began). So, he suffered. Bess later said he was so wretched, she feared he would leap overboard to end the misery.

Once landed, the Houdinis began beating the pavement looking for auditions

Houdini and Mrs. Houdini five years after their runaway marriage

The Houdinis in Europe.
LIBRARY OF CONGRESS, LC-USZ6-2100 DLC

and bookings. Their success was hindered, however, by other performers who had recently disappointed London audiences. One escape artist had failed miserably and embarrassed the theater; a "bullet-proof man" had died when he was shot onstage by accident; and Annie Abbott, the Little Georgia Magnet, had been exposed by revelations in the press that the reason five men couldn't lift her was simple physics and not her supernatural powers.

So Harry had to convince Londoners that he could entertain an audience successfully. The managers he spoke to were skeptical until he met a young fellow named Harry Day, who was filling in for his supervisor. Day doubted Harry could actually escape any cuffs put on him. "If you can get out of Scotland Yard's cuffs, maybe we'll do business," he told Houdini.

That seemed to be Harry's golden moment—of course he couldn't wait to get in touch with Scotland Yard, London's police force. He loved doing police department challenges because they garnered so much publicity for his show. Scotland Yard, if they would cooperate, would put him on the map—or at least on the London stage.

He made an appointment with Superintendent Melville at Scotland Yard the next day. Melville didn't believe Houdini could escape their handcuffs. He snapped a pair on Houdini, with his arms around a column in the foyer, and went off to his office with some other policemen. To their shock, Houdini was free and met them as they opened the door to the office. They were stunned. London's Alhambra Theater immediately booked the Houdinis for two weeks.

Houdini's stint at the Alhambra was a smash. Audiences filled the house every evening for two months. Challengers brought in handcuffs to most shows, hoping to get the advertised reward and beat Houdini. None succeeded. The London booking ended only because Houdini was scheduled to open at the Central Theater in Dresden, Germany. He was signed to work there for a month, on the condition that the first evening's show was successful. If it wasn't, he'd be back on the road.

The first night in Germany, he struggled to talk to the audience in their own language. He'd learned German from his parents while growing up, because it was the only language they'd spoken at home. He wasn't sure how the act was going over, because German audiences at that time didn't hoot and whistle like the American audiences he'd played to in the past. The crowd sat silently, watching him emerge from his box after the first handcuff escape. Then, as if they were one, the audience rose to their feet, clapped, cheered, and stamped. It was a hit!

Houdini's show filled the house every night, and the ticket sales broke all records. The theater manager begged him to stay on another month, but meanwhile other theaters were eagerly scheduling the act. Houdini went on to the Wintergarten in Berlin, where the city had already been plastered with posters telling simply:

WINTERGARTEN

HOUDINI

IM

OKTOBER

The show was a hit in Berlin, too. Tickets sold out ahead of time—the police and fire departments even came to be sure nothing got out of hand. Houdini bathed in the attention, clipping out some of the glowing newspaper stories about his act and mailing them to everyone he knew back home.

Harry's only problem in Europe was that he was only one man, and he couldn't be everywhere at once. The theaters

clamored to get him scheduled, and when they couldn't, they began hiring imitators. Performers with fake handcuffs sprang up like mushrooms, getting attention in Houdini's shadow. Harry realized they were both a threat and a drain on audience attention—after all, if someone paid to see a poorly done escape act, they might not pay again to see his. He decided since he couldn't stop the imitators, he would join them.

Harry wired a telegram to his brother, Dash, who had worked with him in the Houdini Brothers act, before Bess and Harry married. He urged Dash to come over to perform in Europe, telling him:

Come Over The Apples Are Ripe

Dash didn't hesitate, since his own career was going nowhere in New York. He took passage on the next available ship and set sail for Germany. When Dash arrived, Harry had already assembled a set of props for him. He taught Dash the secrets and set him up doing the identical act. To make the most of his Houdini connection, Dash needed a name slightly like Houdini's, and the two of them came up with the name Hardeen. Dash would remain Hardeen for the rest of his career, following his brother's footsteps in magic.

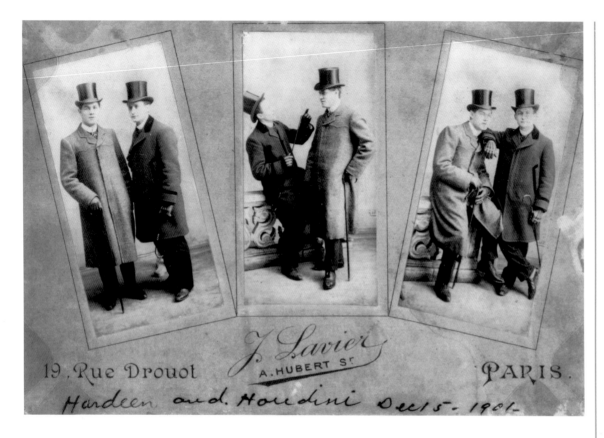

19, Rue Drouot   A. Hubert Sr.   PARIS.

Hardeen and Houdini Dec 15 - 1901 -

Harry's brother Dash, once part of the Houdini Brothers act, became Hardeen, and began working as a competing act—at Harry's invitation.

ner the market on magic escape acts. Houdini hated rivals, yet he believed that Hardeen was really his own creation.

Actually, Hardeen, or Dash, gave many ideas to Harry. Hardeen was never as popular or successful as Harry—only the real Houdini could capture audiences completely. But he was the one who suggested Harry wriggle out of the straitjacket right in front of the audience. Harry had preferred doing his escapes out of sight, so the audience couldn't see his techniques. The straitjacket, however, went over better when Harry was writhing and wriggling free of it in plain sight. It made what had been a boring escape when done inside the box suddenly fascinating when done in full view of the audience. Then no one could accuse Harry of having another person inside the cabinet, helping release the bonds.

Hardeen scheduled performances in Germany while Harry continued across Europe. Back in London, performances once again sold out, with people actually seated on the floor of the stage and hundreds turned away. In the London Hippodrome, 4,000 people crowded in to watch Houdini's act.

One reason Harry was able to garner such attention was because he began

Audiences couldn't get enough, it seemed, and Hardeen quickly made a success simply by copying Houdini. One newspaper reviewed his act, saying he was "the best copy of Houdini in the profession today."

For Harry, having his brother emulate him was soothing to his ego, and it also helped eliminate other competitors. Between the two of them, they could cor-

MAGICIAN'S ASSISTANTS

Magic acts rely on assistants who hand the performer props when needed and move items around on the stage. Bess was always part of Harry's act, both working onstage and sewing costumes. As they became more successful, the Houdinis relied on several assistants, hiring more as the show grew more complicated.

In magic acts, the assistants and performer work as a team, carefully practicing before the performances. Assistants help create distraction for the audience, misdirecting their attention while the magician works through the illusion. Assistants usually appear to be innocently uninvolved with the act, simply handing items, or in some cases pretending to stumble and make mistakes.

Houdini said, "To avert suspicion from our assistants we make them seem as awkward and clumsy as possible. We have them drop things, stumble over chairs, and make mistakes of a minor nature. We want you to get the idea that these men play no real part in the performance of our tricks; whereas, of course, they are the most important cogs in our work."

Houdini's assistants were also expected to keep people out of the back of the stage during the act so no one could view any secrets. It's said that anyone trying to push themselves into the back wings of the stage area would be knocked out with a blow from an assistant's fist. Assistants also switched handcuffs if a challenger brought one that seemed too impossible for Houdini to escape.

Magician's assistants were crucial to success.
MAGIC, ARNO PRESS, 1977 (REPRINT OF 1897 EDITION)

Houdini made up a set of forms for his assistants to fill out and follow, which included directions for packing and unpacking the props, a list of things he required in his dressing room beforehand, and even forms to record the town, the theater, and notes about how the performance went and any complaints or billing problems. He kept lots of written records and studied them in order to decide whether to continue doing a particular act or whether to return to a town or theater.

promoting his escape acts more dramatically. Once he built up the audience's emotion, he would push them even farther to get them wondering if he would fail. He deliberately took a long period of time before reappearing onstage after escapes—sometimes he was backstage reading a newspaper for a few minutes, letting the audience think it was more difficult for him than it really was. He'd rush out, breathless and doused with water, making them think he'd sweated his way out of the cuffs, ropes, and cabinet. His ability to keep the audience on the edge of their seats made his somewhat ordinary performances—handcuff escapes—into dramatic events.

Those first years in Europe were thrilling—and exhausting. Harry did all his own bookings, recordkeeping, and publicity. His only stagehand was Bess. He was wearing down. In 1901 he wrote to a friend, "I am not well. The perpetual worry and excitement are taking a toll on me and I am afraid that if I don't take a rest soon I'll be all done up. You know for the last 11 years I've had the same strain over & over day in & day out & before this luck streak I had to do 8 to 12 shows a day." It was in Germany that Harry hired his first assistant, Franz Kukol.

Kukol was a musician and mechanic and was loyal to Houdini for years.

Escape acts were very popular in European countries where people feared the police. Harry said, "It does seem strange that the people over here especially Germany, France, Saxony, and Bohemia fear the police so much. In fact the Police are all Mighty, and I am the first man that has ever dared them, that is my success." Harry and Bess toured Europe successfully for five years.

ADVENTURES IN RUSSIA

In Russia, where police were a common presence, Houdini found himself walking on eggshells, careful to not attract their attention or break any laws. Police took a photograph of him for their records and seemed to follow him everywhere. His baggage had been thoroughly searched upon entering the country, and he'd needed to get a special permit to bring in his trunk of tools—they raised suspicion that he was a burglar.

His first appearance in Russia was in Moscow, and he practiced with an interpreter to learn enough Russian to speak his own introduction. While he was in a city park practicing his lines out loud, he aroused suspicion and was arrested and hauled off to the police station. Perhaps it was because he was practicing his act in an empty city park. He belted out, "I defy the police department of the world to hold me," to an imaginary audience as he practiced for the evening's performance. "I am Houdini, the greatest of the jail breakers and handcuff kings!" He always used such exaggerated language when he challenged the local police in order to get publicity in the newspaper. But in Russia, such announcements didn't garner enthusiastic audiences, they raised suspicion from the police. He remained under arrest until the stage manager, worried he hadn't appeared for the show, began looking for him.

But Harry wasn't one to let that time in the police station go to waste. While there, he convinced the police to let him try making an escape, just as he had done in the United States and with Scotland Yard in England. Harry had seen prisoners being transported through the streets, hauled off to Siberia in special black jail carriages called *carettes*. Harry convinced the police department to let him try making an escape from a locked *carette*. He described it as "a large, somber looking wagon very like a large safe on wheels." It was a big, black, boxlike structure in which prisoners could be locked and transported. Like a jail cell, it was impossible to escape from. Houdini realized it was a perfect challenge for his skills.

The police agreed. At the designated time, Houdini met the police and was searched from head to toe, without clothing. The *carette* in the prison yard was searched, too. Then Houdini's wrists and ankles were locked into iron bands attached to a metal bar secured with padlocks. He was lifted into the carette and the door locked behind him. Only after the door was sealed was he told that *carettes* were special—one key was used to lock them and another to open them. No one in Moscow had a key to open the *carette*'s lock. To prevent escapes during transport, the vehicles were locked upon departure and could only be opened when they arrived in Siberia. If Houdini couldn't escape the *carette*, he would have a long ride in it to Siberia, and the other key. Houdini then asked them to move the *carette* so that the side with the door, which had a tiny window in it, was away from view, facing the prison wall.

Observers waited. Harry didn't know it, but police observers were stationed at windows above the courtyard, using binoculars to watch him below. About

half an hour later, Houdini walked out from behind the *carette*. The door was still locked; his shackles were inside on the floor of the wagon. The police searched Houdini again, and even made his assistant, Franz Kukol, strip to be searched, too.

The police chief was furious. He refused to sign a statement that Houdini had indeed escaped the *carette*. Of course the police had not allowed any newspaper reporters to watch the event.

Despite the police department's lack of support, word spread. Everyone seemed to hear about it, making it "the biggest sensation that has ever been up here," Houdini said. He used the event to gain more attention, and his nightly show was so popular it was extended another month.

How did Houdini escape from the *carette*? Some think he worked a tool through the tiny window on the door and was able to open the lock about 30 inches below. Others say he hid a metal cutting tool inside the *carette* or on his body, then used it to cut through the floor, remove the wooden planks, and step out, replacing everything behind him. No one is sure, but the likeliest theory is that he smuggled a tool inside. It's likely he used

one of his common tricks for hiding a tool on his body. Although he and Kukol had been searched completely naked before the stunt began, he probably outwitted them by using a fake finger. One thing the policemen failed to notice as they combed over Houdini's body was that he had six fingers on one hand! Houdini had hidden a specially made, flesh-colored, hollow metal finger in his pants pocket while police searched him above the waist, which included looking between his fingers. Then, when he'd taken off his trousers for the below-waist search, he'd slid his hand into the pocket and slipped the fake finger in place. Inside the false finger were special tools: a tiny metal cutting tool and a strip of jagged wire, which acted like a saw when it was pulled back and forth against a surface.

Inside the *carette* Houdini had slipped out of the handcuffs the police had snapped on him, then used the tools hidden in the sixth finger to saw through the floor. He peeled back the metal lining and cut through the wooden boards, sawing them at an angle. As soon as an opening was big enough, he slid through it, then reached back to pull the metal and wooden pieces into place behind him.

Houdini remained in Russia, his show running for several months. He was a sensation with the public, who resented the iron-bound police presence of the ruling czar and his family. Watching a man escape authority, as Houdini did, was entertaining, even inspiring to the audiences. Harry was watched by "spy detectives" during his stay, and he worried he might be arrested for something and sent off to Siberia, never to be heard from again.

Surprisingly, Houdini was very popular with Russia's ruling family, the Romanovs: Czar Nicholas II and his wife Empress Alexandra. The empress adored him. She was a follower of the occult and supernatural and welcomed Houdini to the palace.

The czar and his wife had four daughters and a young son, Alexei. Alexei was born with hemophilia, an inherited disease that prevents blood from clotting normally. Even tiny injuries led to unstoppable bleeding. Physicians had been unable to help him, so the empress turned to Spiritualists to cure her son.

Harry's Russian performances, like those in the rest of Europe, were so puzzling to people that many believed he had supernatural powers. Metamorphosis and his escape acts made people think he could dematerialize, breaking himself into particles, then put himself back together. After one of his Moscow performances, a newspaper said, "Mr. Houdini was able to turn into a woman, then turn into a baby, then come back to his regular appearance." Russians thought he must be a *wolshebnik*, or miracle man.

A miracle man was exactly what the czar and empress needed. Not only was Alexei's health a problem, the country was in turmoil and their future uncertain. Russians were growing discontented because the wealthy refused to improve the condition of the growing number of poor people, and the people were growing angry with the nation's government. The Romanov family, isolated in their palaces, were beginning to worry.

The czar and empress consulted unusual people with bizarre behavior whom they believed were somehow special or could predict the future. Homeless vagrants and mentally ill people were brought to the palace for consultation. Nothing seemed to work. When they learned of Houdini's sensational feats—escaping and rematerializing—they thought he might be supernatural. They summoned him to the palace immediately.

Rasputin was a fake spiritualist who became the Romanov family's advisor after Houdini turned down their offer. Here he is shown surrounded by other admirers.

Houdini amazed the family. The czar and empress asked him to remain with them, working as their advisor. Harry was flattered but turned them down. He wanted to be a showman to the world—not a best friend to the rulers of Russia. He said, "The Empress with her love of mysticism refused to believe that there was a scientific and mechanical explanation for my magic. The Empress begged me to stay and give her the benefit of my gifts, but I refused."

Houdini finished his scheduled performances in Russia. He had made a tremendous amount of money compared to his American earnings, yet was ready to leave the country. "After you leave Russia, you feel as if you had yourself come out of some sort of mild prison." Perhaps his attitude was colored by the fact that he was Jewish, and Jews were forbidden to enter Moscow. To gain travel papers, Bess had filled out the passport forms claiming they were both Roman Catholic. In spite of his popularity with audiences, Russia held no charm for Houdini.

Just after Houdini's visit, the empress discovered a fraudulent Spiritualist, Grigori Rasputin, who claimed to be able to heal the young prince. Rasputin was a wild-eyed peasant who began taking control of the Romanov family and trying to influence government. His power grew, and government officials resented his control of the czar's family. They invited Houdini to return and expose Rasputin as a faker, but he turned them down. A short time later Rasputin was murdered by one of the royal relatives. The czar contacted Houdini again, begging him to come to Russia and be his personal advisor. Houdini declined. He felt the czar was "as helpless as an infant" and had no interest in working with him. Houdini felt the Russian government needed to be reformed but doubted the aristocracy would accept that. Houdini said, "Any radical change would mean that too many grand dukes would lose their jobs." In 1916 the public's anger in Russia boiled over, and revolution broke out. The czar was forced out of power. In 1918 the entire Romanov family was executed by the new Bolshevik government.

Harry was not very interested in politics, but even before he went to Europe he had begun to hear stories about Europeans' growing resentment of Jews. He discovered it was much worse in Russia. Jews weren't allowed to enter the city of Moscow, and it was illegal for

Jewish performers or musicians to perform in theaters. Jews couldn't attend performances, either. While he was in Russia, a two-day massacre of Jews occurred in a provincial city. A mob killed 47 Jews and wounded 500. Houdini visited the site, writing that he was horrified and that "nothing like it could occur in any country but Russia." He learned of a similar incident in another city and discovered that it was censored from the newspapers so no one would know about it. One of the grand dukes he entertained during his tour had expelled 20,000 Jews from Moscow a short time before Houdini arrived. Not knowing Harry was Jewish, the duke had delighted in Harry's show and even gave Bess a personal gift, a small white Pomeranian dog they named Charlie.

When the Russian tour ended, Harry and Bess went back to London. There Harry spotted a lovely gown displayed in a shop window. A sign next to it stated the dress had been specially made for Queen Victoria, who had just died. He knew it was perfect! He went inside and purchased the gown, promising the shop owner it would never be worn in the British Empire, then rushed to the hotel and wrote a letter inviting his mother to

come for a visit in Europe—the gown was just her size. Now he had money to spare and could treat her like a queen. Harry had been sending money every week to Mrs. Weiss, just as he had promised his dying father.

Before heading out on his next tour of European cities, Harry arranged for his mother to visit Hungary—the land she had left years earlier when the family emigrated to the United States. When his mother arrived in Europe, she was able to watch her son perform and enjoyed being the center of attention at a special party he held in her honor in Budapest, Hungary. Harry invited all the Weisz relatives; after all, he was now in the old country where his parents had grown up and he had been born. For two days, they enjoyed a life of luxury and fun, then Cecilia departed to go back to New York and Harry was back to performing for adoring audiences.

While in Europe, Harry began to enjoy real celebrity fame. For the first time in his life he had enough money to buy whatever he needed or even indulge a whim. He was famous enough that important people were eager to meet him. And he was only 26 years old. In about a year's time he had gone from performing at the run-down bottom of show business to the grandest stages of Europe.

STUDENT, EXPERT, WRITER

So how did Houdini indulge his newfound celebrity? He began looking for relatives of his hero, Robert-Houdin, traveling to the long-dead magician's grave, where he placed a wreath to honor the man. Family members were cold to Houdini, and ignored or rebuffed him. That disappointed Houdini immensely. In his search, he did meet people who knew a lot about the history of magic, and one craftsman who specialized in stage props revealed to him how Robert-Houdin had borrowed many of the tricks he claimed as his own from other magicians. That set Houdini to finding out more about the history of magic.

Harry became so obsessed with finding out about history that he began spending all his spare time browsing old bookshops and visiting museums. Houdini found that most illusions had long histories, having been adapted and perfected by each generation of performers. He interviewed people, began collecting old posters and photographs, and started accumulating what would become the world's largest collection of materials about the history of magic. No matter

how much stress he encountered in his career from that point on, he could relax and enjoy himself while reading old books about magic and magicians of the past.

In 1906 Houdini began another career, as a writer. His interest in magic pushed him to share his knowledge with others, so he created a magazine, *Conjuror's Monthly*. He edited and published it for two years. Spurred by the magazine, he began writing books, too. His first, *The Right Way to Do Wrong*, told the secrets that frauds and criminals used to fool the public. Using articles he wrote for the magazine, he created two more books, *Handcuff Secrets Exposed* and *The Unmasking of Robert-Houdin*. He had the help of secretaries and a hired writer (after all, Harry had very little formal education), but his writing projects were nonetheless grueling and he spent many days and nights buried in reading and research.

"Wrote until 2:30 A.M. on the Houdin book. This is a labor of love. I shall be happy when it is finished as it will take a lot of worry off my mind," he noted in his diary.

Houdini was not completely happy with the book once it was published. In it he revealed that Robert-Houdin hadn't

JEAN-EUGENE ROBERT-HOUDIN

Harry Houdini would have remained Ehrich Weiss if he hadn't read Jean-Eugene Robert-Houdin's book about his life as a magician. Robert-Houdin lived in Europe, performing magic acts in theaters during the 1840s and 1850s. Before Robert-Houdin, magicians had performed at country fairs or on street corners. He turned magic into a spectacular entertainment.

Robert-Houdin adopted the high technology of the day, using mechanical figures and small machines in his act. His early training as a clockmaker gave him the skills to design and create small machines that could move, called *automata*. He made mechanical devices that wrote, played musical instruments, and did acrobatic stunts.

He was one of the first people to harness the idea of electromagnetism. He used it in a trick in which a metal chest was placed onstage. Any volunteer could pick it up easily. When he stepped on a hidden button, an electrical charge surged to a hidden electromagnet under the floor. That turned on the magnet,

Jean-Eugene Robert-Houdin.
PANORAMA OF MAGIC, DOVER PUBLICATIONS, 1962

which held the trunk tightly to the floor. No one could pick it up, no matter their strength. He wrote, "The phenomena of electromagnetism is wholly unknown to the general public. I took very good care not to enlighten my audience as to this marvel of science."

Robert-Houdin was hired by the French government to travel to Algeria, a French colony at that time. Algerian magicians were encouraging the people to join in a rebellion against the French government. They were performing glass eating and fake healing to make the people believe they were stronger than the French authorities. Robert-Houdin was sent to demonstrate that the French had greater powers than the local magicians. He performed the electromagnetic trunk trick, making the trunk easy for the French volunteers to lift, but impossible for the Algerians. He even added an electrical shock to the handle when the Algerians touched it.

A Sword Swallower.

SCIENTIFIC AMERICAN, REPRINTED IN PANORAMA OF MAGIC, DOVER PUBLICATIONS, 1962

have been *History of Magic from 1800 to 1850.* In this way it would have shown Magic as it ought to have been known," he explained.

Houdini was fascinated by the tricks and techniques other magicians developed in the past. From his collections as well as years spent talking with other performers he figured out how most illusions were created. In his books and magazine writings he described the famous magicians and illusionists from the past, then revealed to readers the secrets behind the trick.

He wasn't revealing anything new to magicians because most already knew the inner workings of the profession. Secrets and tips were handed down from master to apprentice, parent to child, or purchased from retiring performers.

Houdini's books didn't reveal any of the valuable tricks of the trade at that time. He did tell how illusions had been performed in history, which readers found fascinating. Feats like fire-eating and sword swallowing had been thrilling audiences for centuries, and Houdini revealed the secrets.

Houdini described how sword swallowers usually swallowed a sheath before the performance, and simply pushed the

been the creator of all the illusions he'd performed. That had come as a surprise to Houdini at first. As time went by and he read more about magic history, he realized that the field was one of borrowing and adding to the work of others who had gone before. Later he realized he had been on the wrong track with the book. Even the title was wrong. "It ought to

sword's blade down into it during the act. The sheath prevented the blade from slicing the throat, and could be pulled back out later. Of course, accidents happened. One sword swallower died after a blade snapped off its handle and couldn't be pulled back up out of the throat, making the sheath impossible to remove.

Fire-eaters had performed as early as the Roman Empire, when tales described men who could spew flames out from their mouth. The feat puzzled observers for centuries. It was really a simple trick, as Houdini revealed. Holes were made in both ends of a nutshell, it was filled with sulphur, then lit. Held in the side of one's cheek, the nut could be held between the teeth as the performer breathed in through the nostrils and out through the mouth. The air current would send flames and smoke out of the mouth, in an impressive feat. Over generations, fire breathing became more polished, as some used smoldering balls of flax or hemp to fool emperors and priests into thinking they held superhuman, even sacred, powers.

Other tricks used by fire-eaters included setting fire to a plain piece of paper by simply blowing on it. The secret was that the magician spit a mouth full of phosphorus on it as he blew. The air current

Fire-eaters performing in Paris.
PANORAMA OF MAGIC, DOVER PUBLICATIONS, 1962

caused the phosphorus to ignite, setting the paper on fire.

Other tricks included painting the inside of the mouth with certain chemical concoctions, as well as hardening hands and feet with chemicals so they wouldn't feel pain, allowing one to walk on or handle burning coals. Another technique that allowed fire-eaters to "drink" boiling liquid was in using a special cup with a false bottom that actually held the liquid while the performer only pretended to swallow from it.

Houdini revealed plenty of those sorts of old-time tricks and illusions. But he didn't tell people how Metamorphosis worked, or how he performed his escapes.

FRUITS OF LABOR

Success didn't change Houdini's outlook on life or his driving ambition to be the best at whatever he tried. He and Bess continued to live frugally in everyday life, traveling by third class and staying at inexpensive hotels.

But one thing Houdini enjoyed once he had more money was being generous. He always sent money to support his mother, and at times he supported friends—even total strangers—who needed his help. A magician's widow relied on his check

during her last years, and another fellow, whom Houdini didn't recognize when he encountered him, told Houdini he should remember him well—after all, "you have been paying my rent for the past eleven years!" While Houdini was performing in Scotland he was shocked to see so many poor street children barefoot in winter. He bought 300 pairs of shoes and invited the children into the theater to have them fitted.

Houdini's popularity in Europe did not come by accident. He had taught himself to be a promoter, learning years ago from the sideshows and medicine shows that promotion was vital to gaining the public's interest. He read books about advertising and created his own posters, advertisements, and publicity stunts. Houdini would print up thousands of colorful posters, then distribute them in towns when he arrived to do a show. He created small cardboard locks to pass out before his escape acts. He would buy full-page ads in newspapers, the letters screaming at the reader for attention. He even made a large decal of a photo of himself that could be stuck on windowpanes. He wrote and published a little booklet about himself, "America's Sensational Perplexer," which bragged about his exploits. He had

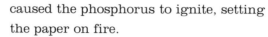

Make a Magic Box

Every magician needs a Magic Box, one of the earliest inventions in the field of magic. Performers have used the same technique to make magic baskets, hats, bags—any sort of container. You'll use it to surprise viewers with your ability to pull something out of the empty box.

MATERIALS

2 half-gallon cardboard milk cartons or similar boxes

Scissors

Black tempera paint (add a few drops of dishwashing soap to make the paint stick to the slick carton surface)

Paintbrush

Tape or glue

Brightly colored gift wrap paper

Cut one carton down to a height of about 6 inches (A). From the remaining carton, cut one of the side sections apart and trim it to 7 inches (B). Paint the inside of the carton and both sides of the flap completely with black paint. Let dry. Fold under 1 inch on one end of the flap. Use glue or tape to fasten it to the inside bottom of the carton. Position it in the center of the bottom (C). Cover the outside of the carton with another color of paint, or glue on brightly colored wrapping paper.

Use the box to perform tricks by hiding items behind one side of the flap, holding it in place with your fingers as you hold the box up for the audience to see there is nothing inside (D). Then slide the flap open and pull out a silk scarf or other hidden item (E).

A white rabbit? Well, maybe!

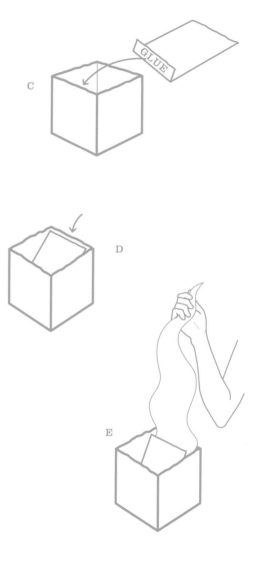

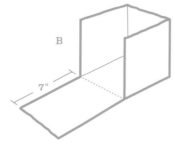

them printed up in batches of 25,000, and gave them out or sold them for a penny. He even came up with his own hand cream, called Zam-Buk, which he advertised and sold as a first-aid lotion.

For one stunt, Houdini hired seven bald men to paint a letter from his name on their heads, sit in a row in a Paris café, and lift their hats one at a time, spelling out the word "Houdini." Harry loved that stunt, saying it "positively stopped traffic." Later, however, he was embarrassed by it, thinking it was too corny.

In June 1905 the Houdinis embarked on a steamer to New York, where they planned to rest up before returning to London for their schedule of fall shows. As soon as they disembarked in New York, Harry and his brothers reunited for a party. Then he set out on a shopping spree.

The first thing Harry bought was a mansion. He plunked down what would be $2.5 million dollars cash today for a four-story house on West 113th Street in New York City.

Crowds gathered by the thousands to watch
Houdini do his spectacular escape stunts. This
is what Houdini saw when he looked down!

5 Going to Extremes

The Houdinis' New York mansion had enough room for the family: Harry and Bess, Harry's mother, his brother Leo, and his sister Gladys. It also had plenty of upstairs rooms for his growing collection of books and magic memorabilia. He once said, "You know, I actually live in a library." He wanted to have his own book collection because it was easier to research and write from his own home. He told his mother, "Someday when I'm too old to perform, I'll spend my time writing about magic. And I won't have to search for source material. It will be here."

He also added some features so he could practice stunts at home, too. He installed a large eight-foot mirror and spent many hours practicing his performance in front of it. One bathroom also held an oversized sunken bathtub. That's where he practiced holding his breath under water, a crucial training regimen for the underwater escape acts he began developing.

Harry also bought a seven-acre farm in Connecticut where they could go as a country vacation retreat. It was named Web Hill and had fields, an orchard, and livestock. He renamed it Weiss Hill and tried to relax there, picking berries and apples. But the quiet life didn't suit him. He busied himself cutting down 20 trees to clear a road and moved several boulders, weighing 200 to 300 pounds each, into a wagon and hauled them off.

He also purchased a large section in a prestigious cemetery, where he began developing the Weiss family burial plot. He paid to have his father's and grandmother's remains—as well as those of an older brother who had died years earlier—removed from where they had been buried and had them reburied in the new family plot. Gruesome as it sounds, he even examined his father and brother's remains before they were reburied, saying he "saw what was left of poor father and Herman. Nothing but skull and bones. Herman's teeth were in splendid condition." Strange as it sounds, for someone who enjoyed dangerous challenges he was always concerned about death, often visiting cemetery gravesites of former magicians and other important people.

Although they could afford to, the Houdinis didn't live extravagantly. Aside from purchasing the home and farm, Harry continued to spend little on luxuries and often dressed shabbily. He saved money, putting what he could in the bank. "Enough to buy a *few* umbrellas for rainy days," he explained.

By autumn, Houdini was back at work, reintroducing himself to the London theater circuit after his resounding success in Europe. He created even more sophisticated escape acts to bring in the audience, and they came by the thousands, packing theaters and filling streets outside. His popularity soared. Crowds stood outside theaters, unable to get a seat, stopping traffic. He was earning almost a quarter-million dollars a week. When his tour ended, he was given a send-off, carried in the air by a cheering crowd, chanting, "And when you go, will you no, come back?" It brought tears to his eyes.

He wrote in his diary: "Pretty good for Dime Museum Houdini."

CONQUERING AMERICA

When Harry and Bess returned to New York they'd been gone five years. They were no longer dime museum players, living hand to mouth and hoping to garner tips from the audience. Harry was now an international star. Yet while he was a star in Europe, he wasn't well known in the United States. People had forgotten him, and lots of imitators had copied his act in Europe and introduced it as their own in the States. He and his brothers spent years trying to expose and destroy the many imitators who pretended to be Houdini or claimed they had invented his tricks.

Men and women did copycat handcuff escapes, and did them so badly they threatened to sour audiences for the real Houdini when he came to town. Copyists used fake handcuffs and other gimmicks that the audience identified as fraud, and it infuriated Houdini. He hired lawyers and sued, and sometimes disguised himself as an old man, with a wig and glasses, and stood up during shows to expose

"We can never tell what is likely to happen."—HOUDINI

fraudulent copyists, such as "Boudini," and others.

To build a name and reputation for himself, Harry returned to what worked: jail escapes with plenty of newspaper coverage. He escaped from jail cells in Brooklyn, Detroit, Cleveland, Rochester, and Buffalo. In Washington, D.C., he set up an escape from one of the precinct jails. Stripped and wearing handcuffs supplied by the Secret Service, he freed himself from a locked cell, then unlocked an adjoining cell where his clothes were stored. He did it in 18 minutes.

From there, he set up the ultimate escape of the day. He announced he would escape the locked cell that had held Charles Guiteau, the assassin who had murdered President Garfield. Guiteau had been hanged for the crime in 1882. Harry went to the location, Murderer's Row, examined the 17 brick cells and the seemingly impenetrable room, Number 2, that once held Guiteau. A heavily barred door and a lock with five tumblers made it seem impossible to escape. Houdini was elated. It was perfect. Since he had several newspaper reporters along, just in case, he decided to do the escape then and there. He was stripped, his body searched, and then he was locked into Guiteau's former cell. It wasn't empty, however. A prisoner waited there, pending execution for murdering his wife. Ignoring him, Houdini escaped from the cell in a couple of minutes. Then, still naked and with the press and police waiting outside in the office, Houdini went to the other cells, opened doors and put the various prisoners into different cells, mixing them up for the guards. When one told him he was being held for being a burglar, Houdini laughed and chided him, "You're pretty bad at it or you wouldn't be in here!"

Then he dressed and went out to the waiting officers and reporters, telling them, "I let all of your prisoners out."

They jumped up. "But I locked them all in again," he said. It had taken 26 minutes.

The police cooperated with setting up the stunt—after all, they were interested in how to make the prison system more secure. Houdini's ability to escape challenged them to develop tighter controls, so they weren't upset that he had gotten past all their locks. And Houdini presented his jail and prison escapes as public service, as a citizen trying to point out flaws in the system to the authorities.

Houdini's secrets were tools, either keys or small picks, that would push the tumblers and working parts inside locks to get them to open. He would hide the tool in his thickly matted hair. Naturally, that would be the most suspicious place for anyone searching him, so when police searched his body before an escape stunt, he would have a key stuck to the palm of his hand with a dab of wax. He'd suggest the police search his hair first, then when they were finished, he'd run his hands through his hair, seeming to groom it back into place, at the same time, sliding the key into hiding in the hair. At other times, he had a key taped to the sole of his foot. He also had a pair of shoes with hollow heels where tools or keys could be hidden. In many cases he was allowed to put his shoes back on after a body search.

Houdini visited the jail cell before each stunt, looking things over carefully (he was said to have had a photographic memory). He asked to see the lock and key to check how they operated, sometimes using a piece of wax hidden in his hand to make an impression of a key so he could make a duplicate. He might leave a master key behind in the cell, for use later during the escape. He tucked keys into bars of soap, left them in the back tanks of toilets, or stuck them under shelves or benches with chewing gum.

He picked up one secret technique from sword swallowers during his years in the dime museums. He made an egg-shaped container that held small tools. He swallowed it and kept it hidden in the back of his throat. Unless the inspection required him to open his mouth to look inside, it was undetectable. He would cough it up once he was securely inside the jail or cabinet.

In some cases, he relied on a partner with a key hidden in his palm, who would shake hands with him through the cell bars after he was locked inside. The key was transferred during the handshake.

For some of his most dramatic stunts, he was bound with chains and large padlocks fastened across his chest and legs. He brought his own large locks and chains to stunts, saying they would add to the effect because they were so large and heavy. The locks did indeed look formidable. Unknown to the bystanders, however, or even police who inspected him before the stunt, his large padlocks were really hollow toolboxes. Once inside the cell or cabinet, he would pop them open with his teeth or fingers and retrieve the tools hidden inside, which allowed him to pick the real lock on the handcuffs supplied by the police.

> "The easiest way to attract a crowd is to let it be known that at a given time and a given place, someone is going to attempt something that in the event of failure will mean sudden death."
>
> —HOUDINI

Houdini's Milk Can Escape

Even though we know of some of these secrets behind Houdini's escapes, we can never know for sure which one he used at a given time. He had other special tricks too, which he never told anyone. How he performed many of his tricks and stunts remains shrouded in mystery.

DEATH-DEFYING STUNTS

To add to his growing reputation, Harry began to push himself harder and harder to come up with more spectacular stunts. He began training harder, running to strengthen his lungs, and swimming underwater. He practiced staying underwater, remaining submerged in his tub for two and a half minutes. He added pans of ice to the water, making conditions even more strenuous. He was practicing for something big.

His new stunts challenged death by drowning. In one, which he called the Milk Can Escape, he submerged himself in a can filled with water, locked the lid in place, then freed himself before drowning. The other stunt involved doing his famous handcuff escapes with the added danger of jumping from a bridge into a river and wriggling from the cuffs while underwater.

The Milk Can Escape went over well with audiences. He wore only a bathing suit and was locked into a pair of handcuffs as he entered the can. Then the lid was fastened in place and secured with padlocks. The audience waited, holding their own breaths to meet the challenge he threw at them as he went into the can. Franz Kukol stood by with an axe to break the can if necessary. A large, box-like screen was placed over the milk can. Houdini called it his ghost house. It prevented anyone from actually seeing the can during his escape. After just over two minutes, Houdini emerged from the ghost house, dripping wet, his hands flung triumphantly free in the air. The ghost house was pulled aside and there was the milk can, the lid still tightly locked in place with chains and padlocks.

The crowd went wild! How had Houdini done it? While some suspected he had played a clever trick on them, many simply enjoyed the idea that he was superhuman. After all, hadn't several audience members gone onstage earlier to inspect the can before it was filled with water? To fasten the locks themselves? They had watched as the can was filled with water carried in splashing buckets by stagehands. Hadn't they seen Houdini,

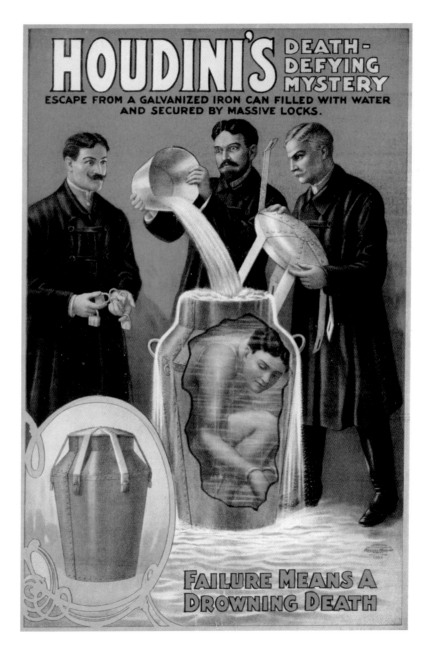

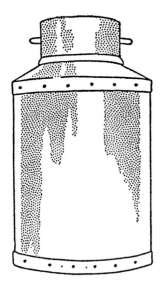

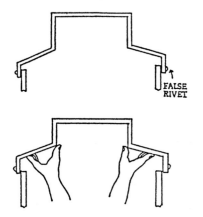

The milk can was gimmicked so it opened by removing a secret fake rivet from inside.

HOUDINI'S ESCAPES AND MAGIC, FUNK AND WAGNALLS, 1930.

wearing only a swimsuit, enter the water-filled can?

Houdini's secret to this escape was having fake rivets fastened around the neck of the can. Once inside, he simply pushed the top of the can up and stepped out. The lid was locked in place, but he didn't need to open it at all. He put the top of the can back in place and opened the screen, revealing everything still locked in place. No one would doubt the rivets around the metal can.

The Milk Can Escape was the beginning of Houdini's new focus on death-defying stunts. No longer just wriggling out of a straitjacket or handcuffs, he raised the bar in his performances to continue thrilling audiences. Pushing himself to develop more creative acts, he realized that defying death brought the most attention. From that point, he moved on to jumping manacled and handcuffed from bridges into swift-moving, even ice-crusted rivers.

He stood high on the Weighlock Bridge in Rochester, New York, wearing two pairs of handcuffs while 10,000 people gathered below, waiting for hours to watch him leap into the swirling black water. Suddenly he leaped. In less than a minute he surfaced, waving the cuffs to the cheering crowd. In New Orleans, he jumped into the deep Mississippi River, then into the Detroit River, the Allegheny River, and the Charles River. He leaped manacled into a lake in Denver, the San Francisco Bay, and into the ocean at Atlantic City. Newspapers blared the stories across their front pages and thousands gathered at each site. In the evenings that followed, his show played to packed houses.

Houdini was flirting with death, and the public knew it. That made him even more famous, and people wanted to be there to actually see him. Would he fail? Copycats tried to make money doing the same stunt and died.

Harry upped the ante, doing more challenges. He escaped out of a packing case, and in another act a piano crate held together by hundreds of nails. In one town he was locked to a door, his hands and feet stretched out and fastened with locks and handcuffs. An envelope company put him inside the world's largest envelope, fastened with rivets, the whole thing tied with ropes and sealed with glue. He escaped a giant football, carried onstage by the University of Pennsylvania football team. He took a challenge from the U.S. Postal Service of being stuffed into a mailbag, the top fastened with a leather strap and lock. A tire chain company challenged him to get out of their product—heavy automobile chains fastened in loops around his head and limbs and across his body. He was chained to two automobile tire rims. He got inside an iron boiler, and the audience watched as it was riveted shut. An hour later, looking worn and tired, he emerged.

While Houdini eagerly took up the challenges because they got lots of publicity in the local newspapers and ensured a big turnout at his evening performances, he studied each carefully before accepting. He turned down offers to drop him at sea locked in a heavy diving suit or to have a huge glass lightbulb blown around his body, which he must escape from without breaking the glass. A plumber challenged him to escape two bathtubs fastened together with iron spikes. One builder wanted to build a brick house onstage, around him, from which he would escape. He wisely avoided anything that might become a death trap. He wanted to challenge death, not die.

The audiences went wild, cheering and screaming when he appeared to take on a challenge. He was trying to top himself, to do harder and more sensational stunts.

Milk Can Escape—
Measure Volume Displacement

Houdini practiced a lot to make this act go smoothly. He practiced measuring the amount of water needed to fill the can up to the neck, so he would know how much his assistant had to bring onstage. He had to figure how much water his body displaced as he got inside the can and the water was pushed out. Water splashing onto the stage had to be cleaned up, of course, so he didn't want to overfill the can, making a needless mess.

He also didn't want water coming up and splashing out through the secret opening around the neck of the can. That would have given away the trick immediately!

Practice the same idea using water and shortening. You can figure out how much space (volume) a solid fills by measuring the amount of water it displaces.

MATERIALS

2-cup glass measuring cup

Water

Shortening

Put 1 cup of water in the measuring cup. Drop in spoonfuls of shortening until the water level reaches the 2-cup mark. The amount of liquid that was displaced, or filled up, is 1 cup, which means you added 1 cup of shortening. Check it out by pouring out the water and pressing the shortening down into the cup. It will level across at the 1-cup mark.

The audience enthusiasm began to push him, and he began to promise "a special sensational stunt at every performance."

Coming up with something sensational wasn't easy. While he tried escaping every imaginable contraption he felt was safe, he needed something new, something entirely different from what anyone else was doing. He needed a stunt that set him apart from any other performer. An idea came to him.

HOUDINI TAKES TO THE AIR

In 1903 the Wright brothers had made their historic first airplane flight at Kitty Hawk, North Carolina. They were pioneers in the growing new field of aviation. Their flight had captured the world's attention and made them household names. Houdini knew he would gain tremendous publicity if he could somehow do an airplane stunt. In 1908 he offered $5,000 to rent the Wright brothers' airplane. He planned to go aloft, handcuffed, then parachute from the plane, escaping from the handcuffs as he fell through the air, landing on the ground safely. The idea was eventually scrapped.

But Houdini's interest in aviation was kindled. Air flight was something thrilling, death defying, and sensational.

Record-setting flights were underway around the globe. Louis Blériot made the first flight across the English Channel and "was the talk of the world and made history," Houdini noted. He had to be part of it.

On a return performance tour of Europe in 1909, Harry and Bess went to the first great air meet, in France. One hundred thousand spectators gathered to watch the earliest airplanes take to the sky. There Houdini hired the best mechanic in France, Antonio Brassac, and headed to Hamburg, Germany, where he purchased the only available airplane for sale, a small Voisin. The proud owner of an airplane, Houdini's next hurdle was learning to fly it.

Houdini performed twice each night at the city's theater, then rushed to the airfield where the Voisin sat in a rented shed. He and the mechanic worked every day, keeping the plane in shape while waiting for the winter weather to subside so Harry could try taking it up for a flight. Finally, one calm morning he started it up. Heading down the grassy airstrip, it tilted downward and the propeller crashed into the ground. Finally, with replacement parts and a bit of decent weather, he was ready to make a flight.

He took it into the air for almost two minutes, flaunting the bright lettering he had painted on its side: HOUDINI.

The Voisin airplane was a biplane, with two sets of wings. It was made of light-weight wood with a cloth cover. The tail and wings were shaped like boxes, covered with the fabric used in hot air balloons. The wings were supported on the ground by bicycle wheels, and two smaller wheels held up the tail. The plane weighed 1,200 pounds. The plane was tied with a rope to a post, and assistants turned the propeller until the engine caught a spark and turned over. When the engine was running fast enough, the helpers untied the rope, unleashed the plane, and it headed down the airfield.

The pilot had little control over the plane; he could make it go up or down a little and that was about it. It was jerky, unstable, and hard to control. The pilot sat between the wings with the propeller and engine behind him. He pushed or pulled the steering wheel to pull a slat up or down on the nose that lifted or lowered the plane. When the pilot turned the steering wheel, it pulled cords connected to the tail, moving the rudder to steer the plane to the left or right. Piloting the plane didn't take a lot of knowledge, just

a lack of fear! Harry didn't mind at all; the Voisin was his and he was flying!

Always competitive, Harry yearned to set a new aviation record, but there were few places where airplanes had not already made a first flight. Australia was the land of opportunity. Other aviators were heading there to try to become the first to record a flight on that continent. Caught up in the excitement, Houdini decided to enter the race, too. He read a pamphlet, "Rigid Stable Aeroplanes," took out a $25,000 life insurance policy on himself, and wrote in his diary, "Hope all will be well with me and my machine."

Houdini loaded Bess, Brassac, and crates full of show props, as well as the disassembled Voisin plane, onboard a ship bound for Australia. Arriving in Melbourne, Australia, in February 1910, Houdini found the summer heat there stifling. "Hottest day I ever lived," he wrote. "Must have been 119-degrees in the shade." Summer in Australia was quite a switch from Germany, where winter weather had hindered his practice flights.

While Brassac set to work readying the Voisin, Houdini promoted his evening performances. He stood 20 feet high on Melbourne's tallest bridge, swathed in thick chains and handcuffs, ready to leap into the Yarra River, with a crowd of 20,000 eagerly watching. It was a "terrible mob," Houdini said. People were run over by a taxicab, and the pushing, jostling crowd forced several people over the bridge railing. As he dove headfirst into the muddy river, he kept his eyes open for sharks.

The performances were a hit. Large crowds paid well to watch him escape from a straitjacket and the milk can and do the old reliable Metamorphosis with Bess. He drove out to the airfield where the Voisin waited, either at midnight for a nap in a tent set up there or at 4:00 A.M. after grabbing a short nap following the last evening's performance. It was a difficult and grueling schedule. It was also the first time Houdini met a task he couldn't perform.

Harry had never learned to drive an automobile. Since 1907, thousands of Ford Model Ts had rolled off the assembly line, and automobiles were no longer a novelty. But for Harry, cab drivers, chauffeurs, and streetcars were easy to find in the city. He traveled by railroad whenever he left the city, so learning to drive an automobile had never been necessary. Now, his awkward schedule made it

difficult to find a taxicab or chauffeur willing to drive out to the airfield in the middle of the night. He took a few lessons from a chauffeur and was able to turn the crank to start an automobile. Harry almost drove the entire trip one night by himself. But he took no liking to it. Flying an airplane or racing a bicycle held appeal, but driving a car just didn't interest him much. It seemed so tame!

The Australian summer weather wasn't as mild as Harry expected. Strong winds beat across the plains, making it impossible to take off safely. Other pilots were faced with the same problem. Everyone wanted to be the first to fly the Australian sky, but the weather wasn't cooperating. "I want to be first! I vehemently want to be first. It is all I ask," Houdini told a reporter.

Finally, after nearly losing patience with the delays, everything was perfect on March 18, 1910. Harry took the Voisin aloft three times that morning. The first flight was short. The plane went up about 25 feet into the air, made a sweeping circle over the airfield, then touched down smoothly. He'd been in the air one minute. The second flight ended with a rough touchdown, and the third was again perfect. The last flight lasted 3½ minutes, soaring more than two miles around the airfield, going at least 100 feet high. Harry touched down almost directly on the spot he'd taken off from. Dripping with sweat, he grinned. Asked how he felt, he said, "never in any fear and never in any danger." He was thrilled. "I can fly now!" he said.

The newspapers ran huge headlines and photographs of Houdini's flight, the first real airplane flight in Australia. Another aviator had gone aloft the day before, at a different airstrip, but had only gone about 12 feet into the air—not even two stories high. Houdini's was a true flight.

He continued making early-morning flights for the next several days, as an audience in automobiles, buggies, and wagons assembled to watch. He moved the plane to a horse racing track, invited the public to watch, and 500 people showed up. Bess and some helpers served them tea and sandwiches.

His flights were terrifying, even by Houdini's standards. The little plane bobbed and dipped in the slightest breeze. It could barely be controlled with the stick-and-cord system attached to the steering wheel, and the little engine was loud but unreliable. Houdini would soar

Houdini in the air! He makes the first flight in Australia.
LIBRARY OF CONGRESS, LC-USZ62-112426

83

straight upward, then a breeze would catch the plane's wings, tipping it over sideways, or heading it nose down in a dive straight toward the ground. The plane was too heavy and underpowered, but Harry pushed the engine for all it would go. Houdini twisted the plane into a loop-the-loop, the wind whistling around him from his spot between the wings.

When Houdini finally touched down, narrowly skimming the tops of the hurdles left on the horse track for jumping events, the crowd breathed a sigh of relief, then went wild with enthusiasm. Cheering, whistling, stamping—the crowd ran to the plane and hoisted Houdini on their shoulders, parading him around the track. A newspaper story said, "Men tossed up their hats; women grew hysterical and wept for sheer excitement, mid deafening cheers and salvos." Houdini said of the death-defying feat, "I made the flight of my life!"

When his performance tour ended in Australia, Houdini wished he "had enough petrol to fly home with my good wife." But the age of cross-oceanic flight was in its infancy—it would be years before commercial flights became the common way to travel. So Brassac took the plane apart, crated it, and they all left Australia, heading home by steamship. Certainly Houdini hated being at sea, still suffering seasickness whenever he traveled. Before embarking, he said, "I saw the steamer yesterday and am sick already. I am certain that I will break all records for being sea sick."

TIME FOR NEW ADVENTURES

The trip gave Houdini a chance to get some much-needed rest despite his seasickness. He had exhausted himself, performing at night and then flying the Voisin all day. "Health in bad condition, not having had much sleep for the past two months," he realized.

Back home, he performed a stint in the United States, then headed back to Europe. He shifted gears again, discarding the handcuff escape act that had been so successful for him. He claimed he would no longer do handcuff acts, and to keep anyone else from taking up the mantle of Handcuff King, he wrote a book that revealed the secrets behind doing handcuff escapes. The book, *Handcuff Secrets*, described all the techniques used by copyists of his act, but cleverly kept from revealing Houdini's own secrets. He explained, "I shall not delve into the very

Build a Box Kite

A box kite is designed to fly higher than most other kite designs. Ancient Chinese and Japanese lore tells of human-lifting kites made long ago. In the 1890s, before airplanes, inventors tried to develop a box kite that could lift a person into the air. The box kite became Wilbur and Orville Wright's model for testing a really big box kite—first as a glider and eventually as an airplane. Houdini's airplane, the Voisin, was built like a large, heavy box kite.

MATERIALS

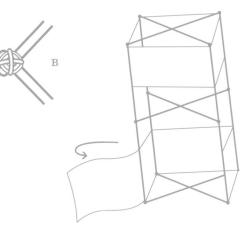

- 6 thin dowels, each 12 inches long
- Strong string
- Masking tape or duct tape
- 4 thin dowels, each 36 inches long
- Wrapping paper or sheet plastic cut 12 inches wide (Large garbage bags work, as does shelf paper, which is 12 inches wide and can be unrolled as needed)
- Scissors
- Strips of cloth for tail

Make the three center interior braces first. For each, take two 12-inch pieces of dowel and make a cross. Tie them together in the center with string, taping over to hold it securely (A).

Butt the ends of the four long dowels to ends of crosspieces at the top and bottom. Tape the ends together securely. It creates a box shape. Then center and tape the middle brace inside the box (B).

Cover the ends of the box frame with a 12-inch-wide strip of paper or plastic. Wrap it around the frame and overlap the ends. Tape securely.

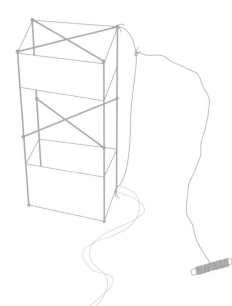

To attach the string, cut a piece about 40 inches long. Tie one end of it to the top corner support and the other end of the string to the bottom end of the same corner support. Then tie the end of your spool of string about 1 inch from the end of the 40-inch string at the top of the kite.

You will need to add a tail so it will fly steadily. Tie a long piece of cloth about 4 inches wide and 5 feet long to the bottom of the kite. If the kite dips and dives in the air, you'll need to add more cloth strips to keep it upright and balanced.

Now all you need is a strong gust of wind!

deep intricacies of some of the great modern feats of handcuff manipulations and jail-breaking, as accomplished by myself."

The book did cause a stir among law enforcement agencies. Police departments claimed to have found copies at the scene of burglaries and condemned Houdini for publishing a guidebook to crime. Parts of the book were banned in Germany, where police thought it gave too much information about how to pick locks. One judge claimed, "It is a book on technical education in the art of thieving." Others claimed it was "a wrong to the community."

But Houdini was busy thinking of even better stunts and acts. "I have tried through many a sleepless night to invent schemes to make an audience appreciate some worthy effort of mine." He was always thinking of new things to try, jotting notes in notebooks and making sketches on scraps of paper. He was always alert for ways to improve his act and do something new and unique. The underwater acts remained the most exciting, because they continued to offer the possibility of Houdini drowning before the audience's eyes.

He thought about being nailed in a wooden box, handcuffed, and thrown over Niagara Falls. His good sense got the better of him and he discarded that idea, opting instead to be lowered in a wooden box from a tugboat in the New York harbor. Handcuffed and nailed inside the box, he was tossed into the ocean. Minutes later, Houdini splashed to the surface, shackles in his hands. Even the magazine *Scientific American* exclaimed at what a miraculous trick he'd performed. His harbor stunt was so successful that he repeated it, gathering 100,000 people to watch him parade down the street, with thousands more lining the wharves and standing in small boats filling the harbor. After 50 seconds, Houdini popped to the surface, and the crowd went wild.

Finally, Houdini was ready to try what many have called his greatest escape. He named it the Chinese Water Torture Cell, and practiced it for three years before performing it in public.

The Chinese Water Torture Cell, which he nicknamed the Upside Down, or USD, was basically a glass box, about as tall as Houdini was. It was filled with water, and Houdini went into it headfirst with his ankles fastened to a pole across the top. Once Houdini was completely in the water, an assistant locked a steel lid in place.

Houdini dared anyone to copy this stunt, warning he would protect his invention in court. But few had the courage to try such a dangerous stunt. "Flying is child's play in comparison," Houdini wrote.

The Upside Down was a huge undertaking. The equipment weighed almost three-quarters of a ton and filled several large wooden crates. The specially built glass box cost $10,000. Onstage, it took 250 gallons of water from fire hoses and buckets to fill the tank. A hole had to be cut in the stage floor to drain the tank after each performance. His assistants used a winch to raise and lower Houdini into the tank. Once inside, the tentlike ghost house cabinet was pulled forward to hide his secret escape techniques, and an assistant stood nearby with a large ax, ready to break the glass box in case Houdini didn't get out in time.

The escape was quick—it had to be. It is impossible to hold one's breath for long underwater, upside down, with pressure building against the lungs. Audiences sat breathlessly silent, then the tent was pulled aside and Houdini burst forward, waving his arms, splashing water all around him. From worried silence to a deafening cheer, the crowd went wild, rising in a standing ovation to cheer Houdini.

Houdini being lowered into the Chinese Water Torture Cell.

It was a smooth trick. So smooth that no one could figure out how he did it. That led many to insist Houdini had superpowers. Spiritualists argued that Houdini must dematerialize and re-form himself again outside the water tank. Historians who have studied Houdini's life and the history of magic still do not know how he performed the trick. It was his most closely guarded stunt.

Houdini was proud of the Upside Down: "I believe it is the climax of all my studies and labors. Never will I be able to construct anything that will be more dangerous or difficult for me to do."

Houdini took time off to attend an international air show in Chicago and was astounded by how quickly the field of aviation had grown. Pilots were staying up in the air for several hours at a time, traveling hundreds of miles in one flight. They were soaring to greater heights than ever, up to a mile in the air. When a stunt pilot crashed after a dive from 3,000 feet in the air, Houdini took part in a fundraiser for the man's widow. He performed the trick he'd wanted to do years earlier before learning to pilot a plane himself. He was shackled hand and foot with cuffs, taken up in the air by another pilot over Lake Michigan, and as

THE WRIGHT BROTHERS

O rville (1871–1948) and Wilbur (1867–1912) Wright were the first to successfully fly an airplane. In 1903 their flying machine was the first powered airplane to successfully carry a person into the air.

They didn't invent the airplane—many inventors around the world were working on similar projects at the same time. They invented a way to control an airplane once it became airborne. Larger planes and powerful engines weren't the route to successful flight. They saw that controlling the level of the wings and banking into the wind to turn a curve—much like riding a bicycle—was essential to controlling the machine.

In 1903 the *Wright Flyer*, their first motor-powered airplane, took flight at Kitty Hawk. The brothers tossed a coin to see who got to go up in it first. Orville won, and he set a world record going 120 feet in 12 seconds, at about 6.8 miles per hour. Wilbur ran along behind one wingtip, in case his help was needed. A bystander snapped a photograph on the camera the brothers had set up on a tripod.

Today, the *Wright Flyer* is displayed at the Smithsonian Museum's Air and Space Museum in Washington, D. C.

LIBRARY OF CONGRESS, LC-DIG-PPPRS-00626

Houdini prepares to jump into the river, arms bound in chains and handcuffs. Thousands of people watch from the bridge.

the plane flew across the lake at about 50 feet, he jumped. He bobbed to the surface, arms and legs free, and swam to shore.

At the air show he met one of the Wright brothers, Orville. Orville and his brother Wilbur had made the famous first airplane flight years before. Orville knew of Houdini's Australian record-setting flight and later went to see his evening stage performance.

Houdini enjoyed the air show, but it convinced him he no longer wanted to fly. He sold the Voisin. "I have had my adventure in the air," he explained.

Back on tour in Europe, Houdini performed in Copenhagen, Denmark, to an enthusiastic audience that included members of the royal family. The next day a telegram arrived, telling of his beloved mother's death back in New York. He fainted after reading the message. When he came to, he was in tears. Harry had adored his mother and had been extremely close to her. While she was living with Harry and Bess in New York he'd spent time taking her shopping or to amusements. He'd written letters to her throughout his life and cherished the letters she wrote to him. Later, in his will he specified that he be buried with his mother's letters tucked beneath the pillow under his head.

Her loss affected him tremendously. Hurrying home to the funeral, Harry departed on the next available ship.

Harry suffered from depression after his mother's death. Eventually he returned to work, going back to Europe to finish the earlier tour.

Back in New York after the tour, he energized his career by doing even more dangerous stunts. He began doing strait-jacket escapes while dangling from his ankles from skyscrapers. Held in the air by ropes and pulleys, the wind sometimes dangerously spinning him toward the buildings, he drew immense crowds on the streets below. In Los Angeles, 25,000 people packed the streets; 50,000 watched in Baltimore; 12,000 in San Antonio. It was dangerous and grueling. "I don't know how long this thing can last," he said. "Some time or another we all grow tired. I have been tired for a long time."

6 Aviator, Actor . . . Spy?

In June 1914, after performing in Germany again, Houdini was on his way back to the United States. He learned there was a famous passenger (besides himself) aboard ship. Former President Theodore Roosevelt was also traveling to New York. He was returning from a trip up the Amazon River in Brazil. Known as Teddy Roosevelt, or simply T. R., he had already served two terms as president of the United States.

Between his usual bouts of seasickness, Harry agreed to do a show for T. R. and a few other passengers. He'd known he would be asked to do a shipboard show, so when he heard Roosevelt was onboard he asked around for information about the man. "I realized that Colonel Roosevelt would be the dominating presence in the audience," Houdini said. "I therefore resolved to work up something which would involve some recent activity of his."

Houdini managed to dig up a map of Roosevelt's trip up the Amazon River, which hadn't even appeared in newspapers yet. He drew a similar map on a chalk slate and hid it behind another blank one. He figured someone—probably Roosevelt—would ask a question related to the former president's special trip. Bess asked everyone in the small audience to write a question for Houdini on a slip of paper, seal them in envelopes, and place them in a hat. Harry picked out Roosevelt's. It asked, "Where was I last Christmas?" Houdini was delighted with how easily the illusion came together. He used "sleight of hand" to slide the blank slate to reveal the "spirit writing" and the map. Roosevelt and the others were astounded. Houdini had made sure the first question he pulled out of the hat was about T. R.'s trip. He had pre-loaded the hat with questions in envelopes, all asking the same question. That way he would be sure to pull the question he was prepared to answer.

The morning after the performance, Roosevelt met up with Houdini when they were out taking morning walks on the ship's deck. Roosevelt put an arm around Houdini's shoulder and asked if the slate writing had really been "genuine Spiritualism." Houdini replied, "No, it was hocus pocus." Houdini later wrote, "It was a shame the way I had to fool him."

WORLD WAR I

Houdini knew war was about to break out, and he was hurrying home. Evidently, Theodore Roosevelt was doing the same thing. In June 1914, just a few days after their steamship reached New York, the opening shots of World War I erupted in Europe. An assassin shot Archduke Franz Ferdinand, the heir to the Austrian-Hungarian throne, igniting a war that had been brewing for months. It was the spark that set Germany, Russia, France, and Great Britain to fighting. The United States, far from the European countries, was not involved.

That December Houdini was invited to perform a private show at the White House for President Woodrow Wilson. It was a high point in Houdini's life. He said, "I have appeared before the rulers of nearly every civilized nation . . . but I have never met so gracious a ruler, so human a man, as the President of my native land." President Wilson must have enjoyed the show. As he was telling Houdini goodbye, Wilson said, "Sir, I envy you your ability of escaping out of tight places. Sometimes I wish I were able to do the same." Wilson had been elected as a president who would keep the United States out of the European war, but as time went by, that was becoming more difficult.

Houdini didn't tell people he was born in Budapest, Hungary. He claimed America as his native land, probably to make sure everyone understood he was a loyal citizen. Hungary joined with Germany in the war, eventually opposing the Allies, which the United States supported. During the war, many people of German ancestry in the United States were suspected of helping the enemy, and Houdini wanted to be sure he was not considered an enemy.

During the war, adult men filled out draft registration cards. The military used the information to draft men into

Houdini entertained Teddy Roosevelt (center) at sea.

THEODORE ROOSEVELT (1858–1919)

A lively outdoorsman and sports enthusiast, Teddy Roosevelt endured a difficult childhood because he was always ill. As an adult he tried to do as much as he could to make up for those bedridden years. He was William McKinley's vice president when McKinley won the presidential election in 1896. After McKinley was killed by an assassin's bullet, Roosevelt became president.

He was a young man with a family, and the six Roosevelt children ran wild in the White House. Pets were everywhere, and it wasn't unusual to see the president and his children playing—roughly—on the front lawn of the White House.

Roosevelt was a popular president because he made many reforms, including enactment of the Pure Food and Drug Act, which cleaned up the nation's food and medicine. He founded the nation's National Park System, the Forest Service, and other conservation efforts.

After leaving the White House, Roosevelt traveled. During a trip to South America he explored the Amazon River basin of Brazil. The trip was grueling, and at one point the usually brazen Roosevelt was so sick that he told the others to leave him behind in the jungle to die. They didn't, of course, and he recovered, returning to the United States.

When he returned, he decided to run for president again, this time creating his own political party, the Progressive Party, which people called the Bull Moose Party. He lost the election in a three-way race, and Woodrow Wilson became the next president of the United States.

President Theodore Roosevelt.

FAMOUS AMERICANS, DOVER PUBLICATIONS, 2005

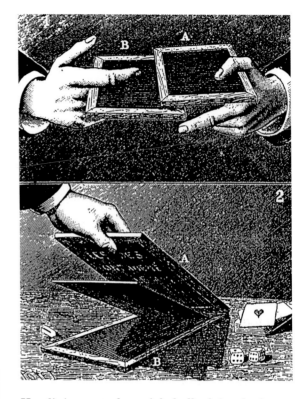

Houdini swapped special chalk slates during the trick, an old magic trick that always amazes the audience.

MAGIC, ARNO PRESS, 1977 (REPRINT OF 1897 EDITION)

the army when more soldiers were needed. Houdini said he was born in the United States on his card and signed it as Harry Handcuff Houdini. He was not drafted because he was now 44 years old, and the war was over before men his age were needed to fight.

Touring Europe during the war was impossible, so Houdini turned to supporting the war effort at home. He organized benefit performances, giving all the proceeds to the Red Cross. He staged many performances for the troops and sold liberty bonds to help finance the war. By the end of the war, he had sold $2 million in bonds to help the effort.

When he performed at military bases, he always added his Money for Nothing act, pulling $5 gold coins out of thin air, then passing them out to the soldiers about to leave for the front. He gave away what would be a quarter of a million dollars today in that one act alone. He also spent his own money to build a hospital ward, which he named after his mother.

Houdini did more during the war than entertain and raise money. He also taught his escape techniques to soldiers to be used if the enemy captured them. He taught how to get out of rope ties and handcuffs and how to stay alive underwater in case a German submarine torpedoed a ship.

BACK ONSTAGE

Houdini had to earn every penny of his income from his shows, because there was no way to charge the crowds in the streets

Magical Money Trick

Houdini hid gold coins in his shirtsleeves and pockets, producing them as if by magic to hand out to the troops. Tell your friends you are going to make money appear out of thin air! Sounds pretty impossible, but it's an easy table magic trick.

MATERIALS

   2 coins

    Drinking cup or glass

Hold the cup with two fingers inside the rim. Tuck two coins under your fingers so that no one sees them.

Now show your friends that the cup is empty.

Say a few magic words (such as *abracadabra*), wave your hand or a magic wand over the cup, and let one coin slip from your fingers and fall into the cup. If your friends dare you to do it again, go ahead. You've got the second coin ready!

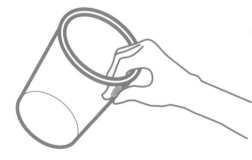

> ## "I have done things I rightly could not do, because I said to myself, you must."
>
> — HOUDINI

to watch what had become a free sample of his work. The daring exhibitions made the news, and created publicity that brought in the crowds. But still, a theater could only sell a limited number of seats, and Houdini still had to perform in every show himself.

If only all his performances were as simple as the one that impressed Teddy Roosevelt! Instead, Houdini was wearing himself out. Dangling from high buildings and doing other large-scale escape stunts was hard work and a continual life-or-death challenge. Houdini decided to shift away from the escapes and do more stage magic. He was famous enough that crowds would fill theaters anyway, and his true love was magic. Houdini came up with some interesting new acts.

Walking "through" a wall onstage was less strenuous but fascinated audiences.

To perform it, Houdini had a secret hole cut in the stage floor, which was covered with a large rug. As the audience watched, a wall was pulled into place on top of the rug. One end faced the audience so they could see both sides. Then Houdini would stand on one side, and two six-foot-tall screens were pulled into place, one around Houdini, so not even a stagehand could see how he did it, and

the other on the other side of the wall. Everyone could see he didn't climb over it or move it. Once the screens were in place, he would almost instantly emerge on the other side of the wall. It was quick, slick, and effective. People even argued that he must have special powers to disintegrate his body on one side, float through the air, and reassemble his body on the other side. He was delighted to puzzle them, but insisted it was really only a magic trick.

To show that walls couldn't hold Houdini, he upped the ante, having bricklayers construct a solid brick wall nine feet tall onstage as the audience watched. As he emerged from the curtain after "walking through the wall," the audience sat still for two minutes—they were so stunned they didn't know what to do. Then they broke out in the usual wild clapping and whistling. Some claimed this was Houdini's best trick ever.

ONE BIG ACT

Houdini always pushed himself to be bigger and better as a performer, and he found the ultimate "big" act—he made an elephant disappear onstage! The fantastic trick was the highlight of a show celebrating the ending of the war.

Houdini's Vanishing Elephant act received lots of newspaper coverage and packed in the crowds. New York City's giant Hippodrome Theater was filled with people when Houdini's assistants brought in Jennie, a 10,000-pound elephant. She wore a blue ribbon around her neck and used her trunk to pick a sugar cube from Houdini's hand. Twelve assistants wheeled in a large box-like wagon. Houdini opened its sides and doors so the audience could see through it. Then Jenny stepped into it, the doors were closed, and in just seconds Houdini fired a pistol into the air. Quickly reopening the doors, the audience was stunned to see the wagon was empty. The elephant had vanished. The audience went wild, of course. Houdini called it "the biggest vanish the world has ever seen." Audiences all over the country as well as Europe and Canada begged him to bring the Vanishing Elephant act to them, but Houdini and Jenny played at the Hippodrome for five months. No one figured out how he did it.

Houdini thought people would rather watch a magician make something disappear than appear—he said, "When you make things appear they say, 'Oh he had it on him all the time!' But when you make things disappear, they are amazed."

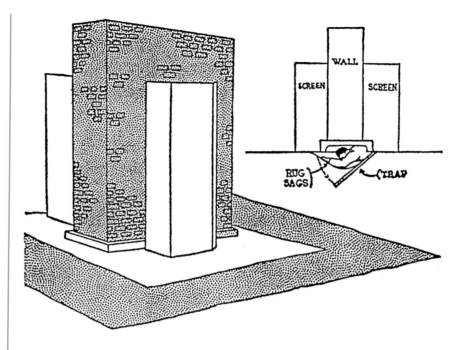

While other magicians made rabbits disappear, he was proud to have made an elephant vanish.

BOBBY, THE ONLY HANDCUFF ESCAPE DOG IN THE WORLD

While performing in California, Houdini met Jack London, the famous author. The two men shared an interest in adventure and dogs and became friends. Jack wrote about wild dogs and wolves facing off in battles for survival in the Far North, and Harry had his own famous dog, a fox

Here's how Houdini did the Walking Through a Brick Wall stunt. The carpet had just enough slack to allow him to slide beneath the wall, through a hole in the floor.

HOUDINI ON MAGIC, DOVER PUBLICATIONS, 1953

Jenny the Vanishing Elephant.

terrier named Bobby, whom he taught to escape from handcuffs. Bobby performed a few times with Harry, once at the annual dinner for the Society of American Magicians, where the professionals thought he was a hit.

Jack and Harry kept in touch, but the friendship ended with Jack's early death. Mrs. London and the Houdinis remained friends for years.

Houdini trained Bobby to escape from ropes, handcuffs, and straitjackets he had specially made to fit the little dog. He was also a "wonderful card dog," according to Houdini, who trained him to do card tricks. In England, audiences knew Bobby as the "greatest somersault dog that ever lived," Houdini claimed.

Loyal and loving, Bobby was Harry and Bess's pet for eight years. Neighborhood children in New York would ring the bell asking to play with Bobby. After Bobby died in 1918, Houdini copied a little poem about dogs into his diary:

> With eyes upraised, his master's looks
>   to scan,
> The joy, the solace, and the aid of man;
> The rich man's guardian, and the poor
>   man's friend,
> The only creature faithful to the end.
>
> (by George Crabbe)

Houdini wrote books about magic and tried to gain some income from them. He bought an interest in a magic supply store and made a little money there. While he couldn't clone himself and perform in more than one show at a time, he did try to profit from the way imitators sprang up to copy his act. He had set up his brother Hardeen as a copycat rival and also hired and trained other performers to do imitation Houdini acts. But there wasn't much promise in trying to expand his act.

Houdini had made himself so famous that his name was a household word. In fact, his name had taken on a meaning of its own. To do "a Houdini," or to be like a "Houdini" meant escaping a tight or challenging situation. It became a popular term, continuing to this day. The word "houdinize," a verb, was added to one publisher's dictionary. But fame didn't pay his bills. He needed to find a way to make money from being a celebrity.

New technology promised to create a way for Houdini to reach larger audiences with less work. Moving pictures projected onto a wall screen, invented by Thomas Edison, were gaining popularity

JACK LONDON (1876–1916)

Jack London was a famous author of Houdini's era. He is most remembered for his bestselling adventure books about dogs in the Alaskan wilderness, *Call of the Wild* and *White Fang*. He was an active adventure seeker, like Houdini, and the two hit it off well.

As a child, Jack discovered the public library, and when he was ten years old a helpful librarian began tutoring and encouraging his studies. He enjoyed reading books about poor boys who grew up to succeed. When he was 13 years old he went to work full time in a cannery. Hoping to improve his lot in life, he bought an old boat and became an oyster pirate. After that, he hired onto a ship and went to Japan. Returning to the United States, he spent a few years wandering the country, from west coast to east and back, riding trains as a hobo and tramp.

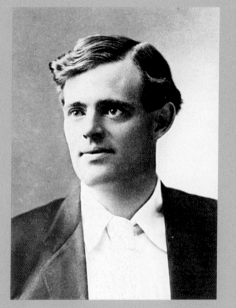

Jack London.
FAMOUS AMERICANS, DOVER PUBLICATIONS, 2005

In 1897 London left for Alaska for the Klondike Gold Rush. He didn't get rich, but he began sending stories about his adventures to magazines. At first they sold for $5, and eventually he was earning $200,000 a year as a writer—a substantial amount in the 1920s.

London bought a 1,000-acre ranch in Sonoma County, California, where he died from kidney disease at the age of 40. The ranch is now the Jack London State Historic Park.

Houdini fought a vicious robot in the movie *The Master Mystery*.

with audiences across the country—and their future looked bright. Most were short films based on slapstick comedy or travel images from foreign lands. Houdini and others knew films could become longer and more complex and would depict real stories.

The first full-length film was *The Great Train Robbery*. It was full of action scenes: men fistfighting, bank robbers beating up a teller, horses galloping in chase scenes, and even fight scenes atop a moving train. Audiences loved the fast pace and action. At the end of the film, an actor pretended to shoot a pistol at the audience. It seemed so real, people actually screamed and ducked! (You can watch *The Great Train Robbery* and other early films online at the Library of Congress. Go to www.loc.gov and search the American Memory Collections for Motion Pictures.)

Houdini knew his action-type stunts would fit well in film. Magic and illusions weren't successful on film because the audience always suspected it was faked for the camera anyway, and there was none of the suspended disbelief that made a live magic show such fun to watch. But the movies were perfect for the kind of spectacular physical stunt work Houdini had invented.

In 1918 Houdini agreed to star in a movie called *The Master Mystery*. He played the role of Quentin Locke, the master detective. Quentin Locke was an early James Bond–type character. Locke battled an evil corporation, International Patents Inc., run by a wicked tycoon from a hilltop castle. The spooky castle was surrounded by a moat and stood on a cliff overlooking the ocean far below. The evil company bought up new inventions to keep them from ever getting to the market. Models of the inventions were locked in the basement of the castle, in the Graveyard of Genius. There was a beautiful girl for Locke to save, as well as a huge, mean robot, the Automaton, to battle.

The movie was a 13-part serial, ending with a cliff-hanger each time to keep audiences coming back for the next movie. Locke (Houdini) battled all sorts of problems and escapes: being bound with barbed wire under a stream of acid; tied with ropes and dropped under a freight elevator descending to crush him; nailed into a box and thrown into the ocean— even an escape from the electric chair.

The films were action-packed and gave Houdini a chance to show off one dramatic escape after another. In other movies he

played the roles of Yar, a Neanderthal; an undercover policeman; and, in *The Man from Beyond*, a man who had been frozen in ice a century earlier. Always, he was escaping evil to rescue a young woman— the role of a romantic action hero.

In one film, *The Grim Game*, he dangled upside down from ropes on the roofs of buildings. In one scene, he fought on a rooftop, suspended by a rope, then freed himself, fell onto an awning below,

In a movie scene, Houdini fights the current near Niagara Falls—his foot is tied to a cable to keep him from actually being swept over the falls.

Houdini clings to a cliff in a scene from *The Man from Beyond*. He pioneered many of the movie stunts we see today.

propeller caught the other plane while in flight, but fortunately they pulled apart before hitting the ground. It was a crash landing, but no one was hurt. The script was changed to include the crash, because the fearless cameraman had continued filming during the whole thing. Houdini did most of the stunts himself. A dummy with a painted face was used in the more dangerous situations, but one summer during filming Harry ended up with seven black eyes and a broken wrist nonetheless.

When *The Master Mystery* finally opened, audiences couldn't get enough. In Boston, 5,000 people waited outside, trying to get seats in the theater. Reviewers raved about the film, saying, "Houdini is honestly a star!"

Houdini loved making films. He and Bess liked Hollywood, where they lived while Harry was filming. The fame he gained from the movies pushed his salary higher when he did live performances. Houdini decided to produce his own motion pictures. He hired a cameraman to film street scenes during his appearances in London and Paris, but had problems with crowds eager to be part of the film. "Everybody wanted to put their face into the camera," he complained. Movies were

rolled off it into the street and beneath the wheels of a passing truck, which he grasped from beneath, and then rode off hanging beneath the truck.

One stunt scene called for him to jump from one airplane to another in midair. While filming the stunt, one plane's

still new to most people, and being caught on film was thrilling to bystanders.

The only part of making movies Harry didn't like much were the kissing scenes. As the hero, he always rescued a pretty girl and fell in love at the end of the story. In real life, he wasn't comfortable kissing anyone except Bess.

Houdini liked his independence and was soon heading up his own movie-making company. The Houdini Picture Corporation made two films its first year. *The Man from Beyond* was about a man frozen in ice for a century who comes to life. The other was *Haldane of the Secret Service*, about the son of a U.S. Secret Service agent who sets out to solve the mystery behind his father's murder. Houdini wrote the scripts, directed the filming, and starred in the movies. When they went over budget, he went back to doing vaudeville shows for two months to pay the bills.

A REAL SECRET AGENT

Houdini liked portraying secret agents in films, probably because it was a bit like real life for him. Until recently, few people knew that Houdini worked as an undercover government agent when he toured Europe in the years just before World

War I. In 2006 William Kalush and Larry Sloman published *The Secret Life of Houdini*, the first book to reveal Houdini's hidden role as a spy. They found many documents proving Harry had begun working undercover with the British police during his first trip to London in 1900. At that time, France, Britain, Germany, and the United States were all spying on one another. Fears of anarchists, people who wanted to overthrow the government, and labor union activists made government officials uneasy. President McKinley had been assassinated in 1898, and several rulers in Europe had been killed or threatened.

When Houdini was performing in Kansas City, Missouri, he had visited the police station frequently, doing handcuff challenges and jailbreaks. While there he was also trained to spot counterfeit money. In 1898 Houdini had met John Wilkie, head of the U.S. Secret Service. A former magician himself who some-times hired entertainers to act as under-cover spies, Wilkie likely hired Harry to do undercover work.

It's likely that Harry began doing undercover work when he visited California in 1899. At that time, the U.S. Secret Service was trying to bust a large

Houdini worked with John Wilkie, head of the U.S. Secret Service.

ring of counterfeiters who had flooded the region with fake silver dollars. The counterfeiters were using a mold made from a real silver dollar, and the fakes were very hard to pick out.

Traveling entertainers like Houdini moved around the country, meeting lots of people and learning about local affairs. As Houdini headed to San Francisco that trip, he had pockets stuffed with silver dollars picked up in evening gambling games with other passengers. He'd been trained to detect counterfeit gold and silver dollars in Missouri and Chicago, and likely was looking for sources making the phony money. Silver dollars had been minted a few years earlier, but that had stopped as the nation fought over whether to back a national currency with gold or silver. Instead of official government dollars, coins made by small western silver mines were flooding into circulation.

HARRY SPIES IN EUROPE

While the Secret Service tried to stop counterfeiters, they also tried to learn about any plots to overthrow the government. Several European leaders had been killed, and in 1901 an assassin thought to be part of a criminal group killed President William McKinley. People feared groups might be plotting against governments in Europe or the United States.

When Houdini visited London, Wilkie had arranged for him to meet with William Melville, the head of Scotland Yard's Special Branch. Melville was in touch with law enforcement officials in France, Germany, and Russia, using undercover spies and informants to find criminals. Melville hired the spy whom the fictional movie character James Bond was based on. He also hired Harry Houdini.

Houdini impressed the Scotland Yard police with his handcuff escapes, and Melville put him to work as an undercover spy. He was perfect for the work because he traveled so much and knew techniques of secrecy and illusion. He could spy on other countries, ones Britain knew were sending spies as well. It was a time of distrust among nations. Britain especially worried that Germany might become a future enemy. Houdini spoke German (his father never did learn English), and as an entertainer he could move easily throughout Europe, wherever he was needed. While in Germany and surrounding countries, Houdini sent information back to Melville in London.

When Harry returned to the United States from a European tour in 1902, he met with Wilkie at the Secret Service, who had been in touch with Melville in London. Harry was home for only ten days, which seems odd considering how much he hated seasickness during the ship travel back and forth. Perhaps he received a briefing or assignment, then was back on tour.

Russia was the center of anarchist plots, and that's where Houdini performed next, gaining trust and access to a variety of people, including the czar's family, the Romanovs, and their spiritual advisor, Rasputin.

Because he traveled to several European countries frequently, Houdini was useful to both the U.S. Secret Service and Britain's Scotland Yard. He spent time exploring police stations, prisons, jails, and security systems in every city he visited—perhaps he could pick up useful information. Because Britain was suspicious of Germany years before World War I started, Scotland Yard authorities relied on Houdini's information gathered from tours there.

While doing his early performance tours in Germany, Houdini visited places like the Krupp Works, an important defense plant. He was invited inside because employees challenged him to escape Krupp master handcuffs. He got out of them in 30 minutes, but a vicious screw in the device injured his hand, which would take years to heal. He also met with an inventor of a compound that could burn a hole through an iron safe.

Houdini and other magicians who worked as covert agents inspired many gadgets and devices that made spying easier. They were ideas that came from doing stage magic acts, refined to meet the needs of under-cover spies: shoes with hollow heels (like the ones he used to hide keys inside), tiny hidden cameras (Houdini created one so his street scenes could be filmed for movies without crowds trying to get in the way), invisible ink, and disappearing ink.

Houdini also exposed various ciphers and codes. While he toured Europe, reporting to Scotland Yard and later to the Secret Service when he returned home, he sent in newspaper and magazine columns about magic and his tour. He may have been sending coded messages in the

The U.S. Secret Service was first created to stop counterfeiters.
U.S. SECRET SERVICE

COUNTERFEIT MONEY

Counterfeit—fake—money has played a major role in history. Because printing phony bills or minting fake coins actually steals money from the national treasury, it is considered a major form of treason. In the past, people were put to death for creating fake money.

During the Revolutionary War, Britain printed up lots of fake currency, hoping to destroy the colonial effort by circulating worthless Continental notes. During the Civil War, almost half the money was counterfeit, both North and South. Besides ordinary criminals, both sides printed up fake money to hurt the enemy's economy. At that time it wasn't hard to create fake money—there were over 1,600 banks printing their own bills, with their own designs. Few people even saw many of the 7,000 different real bills, let alone could tell the difference between real and fake.

In 1862 a national currency was adopted, making only one form of paper and coin money legal. That made it easier to recognize real from fake money. In 1865 the U.S. Secret Service was created to track down counterfeit money. Later, it also protected against counterfeit postage stamps.

In 1901 President William McKinley was killed by an assassin's bullet. After that, the Secret Service began protecting the president of the United States. In 1907 they began investigating theft of government lands in the West, returning millions of acres of land to the government. In 1908 some Secret Service agents were moved from the Treasury Department to the Department of Justice to create what would later become the Federal Bureau of Investigation. When World War I broke out in Europe, President Wilson directed the Secret Service to begin investigating spies in this country. In 2003 the Secret Service was moved from the Department of the Treasury to the Department of Homeland Security.

How to tell a dollar bill is real? The paper is specially made, using bits of red and blue threads in the paper pulp. Look closely at a real dollar bill (any denomination) and you'll see tiny red and blue fibers. A phony bill won't have them.

Today fake credit cards are as much a problem as phony money. Criminals are always trying to stay a step ahead of law enforcement, and new technologies sometimes create opportunities for fraud before the law can catch up.

columns—a practice he admitted to doing through coded classified ads.

Houdini told how he first learned about secret codes:

> My first introduction to the world of cryptography occurred about twenty years ago when, not having enough money to wire home for my return fare, I was stranded with a small touring company in Chetopa, Kansas. I wished to leave that beautiful city as fast as the inventions of mankind would permit me. But alas! I lacked sufficient money with which to buy a postage stamp, let alone railroad fare, so I went to the telegraph office to send a message "collect at the other end." After a long conversation with one of the clerks or operators, he accepted my wire, and I sat down to wait for an answer from Home Sweet Home.
>
> While I was waiting, an old man walked into the office and handed in a message, paid for it, and left the office. No sooner was he gone than the operator called me to him and said, "Here you magician, tell me what this means."
>
> I shall never forget the message; it was of such a nature that it is almost impossible to forget it. The operator looked at me with a smile and said that he would send the message and then allow me to study it while I waited for my answer.

Write an Invisible Message

 ere's a good way to pass a secret message to a friend without letting it fall into the wrong hands!

MATERIALS

Cotton swab or small paintbrush

2–3 tablespoons lemon juice or white vinegar

White paper

Steam iron

To write the message, dip the swab or brush into the juice, and print the message on the paper. Let it dry completely, then give it to a friend. Tell him or her that in order to read the message, he or she must press the paper with a warm steam iron. The heat will bring out the "secret" writing, and the words will turn brown.

Make a Secret
Spy Safe

ou can hide valuables in this secret safe that looks to anyone like just another book on the shelf. Only *you* will know that it's not just an ordinary book!

Adult supervision required.

MATERIALS

Old book with a hardcover binding

Piece of paper or cardboard roughly the same size as the book

Scissors

Craft knife

White glue

Pencil

First cut a pattern template from the paper or cardboard, making it 2 inches smaller all around than the outside border of the book's pages.

Open the front cover of the book, and lay the pattern on top of the pages. Trace around it with a pencil. Use the craft knife to cut along the line, going several sheets deep at one time. Peel away the cut-out section.

Positioning the template in the same place each time, continue tracing and cutting out the rest of the pages, a few at a time, until all the pages have been cut. You've created a hollowed-out center for the book, with the outside edges of the pages looking normal.

Use glue to stick pages together here and there, helping the book to hold a stiff shape.

You can put important notes, tiny items, or even money in the secret compartment you made, then slide the book in among other books on the shelf. No one will ever know it holds a secret!

I was in that office at least five hours, and to that wait I am indebted for my ability today to read almost any cipher or secret writing that is handed to me. I have made quite a study of this art, and often it has been the means of giving me a friendly warning or clever hint to look out for myself.

The message that I studied in that grim telegraph station was written as follows:

XNTQLZCXHM FOKDZRDQDS TQMZRJGDQ SNEN QFHUDE ZSGDQ.

I managed, after some worry, to solve the message, and very few things in later life gave me as much pleasure as did the unraveling of that code. I noticed that by putting one letter for another, I eventually spelled the entire message, which read as follows: "Your ma dying; please return; ask her to forgive. Father."

The telegraph operator seemed to think that this was a great feat, and even while we talked about it the answer arrived:

BZTFGSDWOQ DRRZQQHUDMN NMXNTQKHSSKD ZKHBD

Which reads: "Caught express; arrive noon. Your little Alice."

This is a very simple cipher, and all there is to it is to alter the alphabet, and instead of writing the letter required, simply write the letter in front of it. For instance, if writing the word "yes," according to your code, you will have to write "XDR." Note: it is necessary to use Z for the letter A.

(from *Houdini on Magic*)

It's not clear what information Houdini passed on or if he ever found anything useful. Perhaps, the trickster that he was, he was a covert agent for both sides. We will never know what he was up to completely—that's the mystery of Harry Houdini. He did halt his performances in Europe during the war—few entertainers were working during wartime anyway—and resumed touring Europe again once peace was restored. After the war, Harry didn't seem to be involved in espionage or undercover work for government police agencies any longer.

Instead, he turned to what became a more dangerous type of undercover work—exposing fraudulent spirit mediums to the public.

He became a ghostbuster.

Crack a Secret Code

Secret codes are not only important for spies but also can be used to protect personal information. Bess and Harry had secret codes to talk to each other, and Harry sometimes wrote things in his diary in his own secret code so no one else could understand it.

Before telephones became popular, people sent messages by telegraph. To send a message, you wrote it out on a slip of paper and gave it to a telegraph operator, who put the message onto the wire using taps on telegraph keys. It was quick and efficient—but not at all private. The telegraph operator, others along the telegraph line who relayed the message, and the messenger who finally delivered the written-out message on the other end of the line to the recipient all knew the message. That was a problem for personal messages as well as business messages that were best kept secret. So people often developed simple codes to pass their message via telegram. Here's how it works: For the letter A write Z, for B write A, and so on. Or, change the order slightly and come up with your own personal code!

A = Z	H = G	O = N	V = U
B = A	I = H	P = O	W = V
C = B	J = I	Q = P	X = W
D = C	K = J	R = Q	Y = X
E = D	L = K	S = R	Z = Y
F = E	M = L	T = S	
G = F	N = M	U = T	

Now see if you can crack this simple code:
FNNC KTBJ!

Ghostbuster

Sherlock Holmes, like Houdini, was a celebrity in the early 20th century. Unlike Houdini, however, Sherlock Holmes was entirely made up. He was a detective character in a series of mystery stories that became world famous. Sherlock Holmes—with his sidekick, Dr. Watson—solved spooky mysteries set in gloomy English settings. Everyone knew of both Houdini and Sherlock Holmes, but few knew their paths crossed. Houdini didn't actually meet Sherlock Holmes, of course, but his creator, the writer Sir Arthur Conan Doyle, became close to Houdini in an odd friendship with an unusual end.

FRIENDS AND RIVALS

When Harry Houdini met Sir Arthur Conan Doyle after a performance in England, the two struck up a quick friendship. They were both adventurers interested in history and writing and in the world of the occult and ghosts. Doyle knew Harry missed his dead mother and suggested he attend a séance, where Harry could actually speak to his mother's ghost. While Houdini didn't believe ghosts existed, the thought of communicating with his mother appealed to him greatly. He agreed to attend a séance with Sir Doyle and his wife. It began a new chapter in his life, one that took much of his energy and threatened his very life.

Arthur Conan Doyle, born in England in 1859, grew up in poverty. His father was an alcoholic with mental illness, and his mother had a difficult time supporting the children. He attended Catholic schools and eventually became a medical doctor. When he wasn't seeing patients, he spent his time writing stories. He created a fictional detective called Sherlock Holmes, and his mystery stories became very popular.

His stories and books were so successful, he made enough money to give up practicing medicine and began writing and traveling. After visiting Africa, he wrote a book about England's colonies on that continent. The king of England made him a knight because of the book, and after that he was called Sir Doyle. His wife became Lady Doyle.

Spiritualism was popular during the years Doyle was growing up, and he became interested in the psychic world. He wanted to learn more about spirit worlds and experimented with mental telepathy, mind reading, and fortune telling. He said he believed that "intelligence could exist apart from the body." He thought the soul continued to exist after death and might contact the living. He believed in ghosts.

Like many other parents whose sons died during the war, Sir Arthur Conan Doyle wanted to speak again with his dead son, Kingsley, who had died from wounds and pneumonia just before the war ended. When Doyle sat in a darkened room with a spirit medium named Evan Powell, he thought he heard his son's voice again. When he felt someone put

a hand on his head and a kiss on his forehead, he believed it was his lost son.

Lady Doyle also took up Spiritualism and became a medium. She claimed to be able to go into a trance, during which she would write messages that came to her from the dead. The spirits never contacted Sir Doyle; they only gave him messages through his wife, who channeled them for him and other people. It was called "trance writing" and was said to come from the ghost through the medium.

Séances were held in darkened rooms where a small group of people gathered around a table. They usually all held hands and silently waited as the medium went into a trance, and then they would hear the voices of spirits. Sometimes bells rang, or people felt a hand on their head or shoulder or heard a voice calling their name. The table might rise up into the air. Knocking and thumping sounds were common. The medium said all the commotion was coming from the spirits, who were trying to "break through" and talk with the group.

A successful séance was eerie and supernatural, and people desperately believed it was real. It was also profitable for the medium, who charged high fees and told people they must return for

Sir Arthur Conan Doyle, the creator of Sherlock Holmes stories.

more sessions because the spirits were eager to continue talking with them.

To grieving families like the Doyles, Spiritualism made sense. It became the most important thing in their lives. To magicians like Houdini, it was suspicious. Years before, he had learned of the tricks used by the mediums—in fact, he and Bess had pretended to be mediums when they worked with a traveling medicine show. He knew people who were former mediums who told him how they created the strange effects. As a magician, he resented people using tricks to fool unsuspecting people. Even worse, they believed it as a religion. He began working on a book revealing Spiritualism as a hoax.

That's when he met the Doyles. Sir Doyle had been eager to meet Houdini because he believed the magician really had supernatural powers of some sort and hoped he would share them with him. They exchanged letters, and the Doyles invited Houdini to visit at their English country home.

After Houdini entertained them with a few tricks, Sir Doyle surprised Houdini by telling him how he had visited his dead son six times through a spirit medium. What surprised Houdini more, however, was the revelation that Lady Doyle was herself a spirit medium.

When Doyle saw Houdini perform an escape or illusion, he became even more certain of Houdini's supernatural gifts. To Houdini, Doyle seemed completely gullible. Houdini wrote to a friend that after Doyle watched his performance, "He was so much impressed, that there is little wonder in him believing in Spiritualism so implicitly." Doyle seemed so innocent, so easily fooled.

Doyle told Houdini about some "spirit photographs" he had. Spirit photography was a new idea at the time. New, smaller cameras and film, easy for anyone to use, made snapping photographs popular in the 1920s. When odd shapes and images appeared accidentally in photographs, Spiritualists claimed they were ghosts or spirits accidentally captured on film. Doyle quickly fell for spirit photography, and when someone gave him photos of supposed fairies, gnomes, and a dancing goblin in a forest setting, Doyle believed they were real and protected them in a locked safe. He even published a book about the fairy photos. He knew Houdini would be skeptical, telling him, "A fake! You will say." Undaunted, however, Doyle added, "No sir, I think not. It is a revelation."

Years later, teenagers confessed to having posed the photos using fairy images cut out from the pages of a children's book. They were a hoax.

The Doyles knew Houdini doubted Spiritualism, so they set up sessions with famous mediums, hoping they could convince him. After a few sessions, Houdini was even more certain they were frauds. "This is ridiculous stuff," he said.

HARRY EXPOSES HOAXES AND MAKES ENEMIES

Houdini attended a hundred séances trying to find his mother's spirit, but nothing worked. He was also researching his book, and he figured out the tricks every medium was using. "Nothing new," he wrote a friend. "It is the same old routine."

He was critical and suspicious, and the Spiritualists began to resent him. He made many enemies. His book *Miracle Mongers and Their Methods* had exposed entertainers such as sword swallowers and fire eaters, telling the long-held secrets behind such old feats. The public wanted more—they wanted Houdini to reveal the secrets of the Spiritualist mediums. Even the *New York Times* urged Houdini to take up the project.

The Spiritualists had two reasons to resist Houdini: religion and money. Many believed Spiritualism was a new religion and felt religious freedom should be protected. Mediums claimed their ability to contact ghosts was a gift from God. To say it was a trick was offensive. On the other hand, the mediums were out to make money—charging high fees from clients. It was common for frauds to prey on wealthy people who were lonely or had lost a loved one, working on them until their money was gone. If Spiritualists were revealed to be fake, they would lose substantial income.

In 1922 the Doyles visited the United States to gain converts and raise funds for Spiritualism. Lady Doyle gave séances and did her trance writing. She claimed that Houdini's dead mother, Mrs. Weiss, had contacted her. Houdini was at the séance himself and went away disappointed. Lady Doyle had claimed she spoke in English, while Houdini knew that his mother spoke five languages, none of them English. Worse, during the séance, Mrs. Weiss's ghost didn't mention that it was her birthday—something Harry felt sure she would have mentioned had it really been his mother speaking. He knew it was a hoax. He expected it would be,

"Showmanship is the largest factor in putting an act over."—HOUDINI but he had secretly hoped she really might come back from the dead, even for just a moment.

Houdini made the Doyles mad when he told a newspaper reporter, "My mind is open. I am perfectly willing to believe, but in the 25 years of my investigation and the hundreds of séances which I have attended, I have never seen or heard anything that could convince me that there is a possibility of communication with the loved ones who have gone beyond."

Lady Doyle was furious! She and Sir Doyle fought back. They claimed Houdini had been too nervous during the séance to admit it was real. They claimed Lady Doyle had received a second message from the spirits at that séance.

The second message was that Houdini would die very soon.

Lady Doyle's career as a Spiritualist took off. She broadcast her radio shows to 500,000 people and began writing newspaper articles about contacting ghosts and spirits. When the explorer who led the expedition to open King Tut's tomb in Egypt suddenly died, Sir Doyle claimed it was due to an evil spirit. "There are many legends about the powers of the old Egyptians," he pointed out. Houdini challenged him, pointing out that the

explorer's doctor had said the man died from an infected insect bite. Houdini and Arthur Conan Doyle liked each other as friends, but neither would give up trying to change the other's mind about Spiritualism.

Houdini studied the history of Spiritualism from its beginnings with the Fox sisters in the 1840s. The two sisters lived in a Hydesville, New York, farmhouse and began giving entertainments to audiences by communicating with ghosts or unseen spirits. The Fox sisters knocked messages on a tabletop, and a spirit answered them back. People were fascinated, and the women's popularity grew.

Two men, called the Davenport Brothers, quickly copied the sisters' techniques, creating weird loud noises and table thumping. Eventually an entire movement developed as mediums used their unusual powers to talk with the spirits of dead friends and relatives for paying customers.

The mediums played all sorts of tricks to make it seem they had special powers. One medium could make a ghost type on a typewriter, others made the table move or blew through trumpets. Mediums sometimes spoke in other voices during trances, like a ventriloquist does, or

WINCHESTER HOUSE OF MYSTERY

Mrs. Sarah Winchester is one example of a medium's influence. Her story, like others, is about a grieving person being taken advantage of by a phony medium. While Mrs. Winchester had millions of dollars to spend, many people did similarly strange things after mediums told them they could please the spirit world.

Mrs. Winchester's husband had amassed a huge fortune manufacturing and selling Winchester rifles in Connecticut. After both her daughter and husband died, Mrs. Winchester visited a medium, who told her that ghosts of thousands of people who had been killed by Winchester rifles were angry and seeking vengeance. To remove a family curse and protect her own life, she should move to California and begin construction of a huge mansion. The house would be her home as well as provide a home for the wandering spirits, who would be pleased and protect her from evil forces.

In 1884 she began the project, hiring a team of carpenters to work around the clock, every day of the week—for 38 years! When she died at the age of 85, the house was still under construction. It has 160 rooms, 3 elevators, 47 fireplaces, 40 bedrooms, and 6 kitchens. Stairs lead to ceilings and doors open to nowhere. She had drawn out the rooms as they were constructed, using pieces of paper or even a tablecloth. The rooms were lavishly furnished, with chandeliers and carpeting.

The Winchester House is now a national park site and open to the public for tours. Visit the Web site at www.winchestermysteryhouse.com, or the house at 525 S. Winchester Boulevard, San Diego, California.

Sarah Winchester continued building this house on advice of a spirit medium, believing she would die if it were ever completed.
LIBRARY OF CONGRESS, HABS-CAL, 43-SANJOS, 9-2

began writing words they said were coming to them from a spirit.

Spirit mediums thought magicians were their worst enemies, because magicians easily recognized illusions and how they were done. After all, that's what magicians did onstage, except they didn't try to fool people into thinking they were talking to someone who had died.

While the Spiritualists knew they were tricking people, they kept it a closely guarded secret. The public didn't completely believe mediums could talk to the dead, but the possibility was intriguing.

A growing number of psychics and mediums popped up around the country as the fad spread. After World War I ended in 1918, many people paid spirit mediums to try to contact loved ones who had died in the war. People wanted to believe that there was life after death, and eager mediums tried to please them. Newspapers reported on the exciting possibilities, and Spiritualism's followers increased.

In 1924 *Scientific American* magazine announced a prize offered to any medium who could produce solid proof of contacting ghosts before a panel of judges. Harry Houdini was one of the judges.

As a judge for the contest, Harry easily exposed several fakes. One person rigged hidden electrical wires between a bell and his chair. Another used her head to tip the table over, while holding hands with the guests at a séance in a dark room.

Harry said, "Magicians are trained for magical work; therefore, they detect false moves more quickly than ordinary observers who might witness a séance without knowledge of the subtleness of misdirection."

Houdini easily proved that spirit photography was a hoax. He created fake photographs of himself talking with the "ghost" of Abraham Lincoln. The photo was made by developing two images on the same piece of photo paper. Today that's called a double exposure and seems easy to see, but at that time people were not familiar with photography or film-developing techniques. Even a splotch or mark on a photograph was sometimes claimed to be a spirit caught by mistake.

Spiritualists quickly moved on to more spectacular feats than knocking knuckles on the tabletop or showing blurry photographs. In the 1920s several mediums impressed clients and attempted to prove they were really getting in touch with ghosts by oozing "ectoplasm" from their nose, ears, mouth, or skin. Ectoplasm was said to be the mysterious stuff that oozes out from ghosts and makes it possible for them to materialize and do things, such as lift tables or ring bells during a séance. Ectoplasm looked different depending upon the medium. Some oozed a gelatin-like glob onto the table. Others spit up yards of filmy cloth. Some seemed to spurt out a handlike piece of ectoplasm. Ectoplasm was captured in photographs as a smoky film or blur, or a blob on the table.

Houdini exposed several frauds who had actually chewed up paper or fabric, swallowed it, and spit it up during the séance. He knew very well how they did it because he had learned the technique during his dime museum days from people like the man who swallowed frogs and then burped them up. It had been useful to Houdini—he'd swallowed keys, small tools, and even needles, coughing them back up when needed for some of his tricks and escapes.

But not all frauds were so easy to expose. Perhaps the most famous medium of Houdini's day was a woman who called herself Margery. Her real name was Mina Crandon. She was married to a Boston surgeon, who also participated in the many séances she held. She was a talented magician, fooling even Houdini at times

Make Some Slimy Ectoplasm

Ectoplasm is perhaps the weirdest thing to come out of the Spiritualist craze. Most mediums used a sort of slimy substance that sometimes glowed in the dark. Thanks to phosphorescent paints, things could be made to glow when a bit of light hit them in the dark. Just like the glow-in-the-dark stickers and stars on bedroom ceilings today, the object glowed when the lights went out. Today we're used to such things, but in the 1920s people were shocked and stunned. You can make some slimy ectoplasm of your own.

MATERIALS

1/2 cup white glue

Plastic container with lid or small self-locking plastic bag

Food coloring

1/2 cup liquid starch (found in the laundry section of the grocery store)

Spoon

Pour the glue into the plastic container. Add a few drops of food coloring, and stir to mix well. Gradually pour the starch into the glue, and continue mixing. If the mixture is sticky, add more starch.

When the mixture gets thick enough to handle, begin kneading it with your hands on a kitchen counter, tabletop, or hard surface. Work it until it is smooth and glossy. Cover and refrigerate overnight. This ectoplasm can be pulled and twisted—even cut with scissors. Keep it away from upholstered furniture and carpeting—it can make a mess as it dries.

117

when he sat in on her séances trying to figure out her techniques. She fooled several scientists and professors, who believed that she truly brought ghosts to life and spoke with them. Sir Arthur Conan Doyle was a firm believer in Margery's gifts.

When Margery entered the *Scientific American* contest, claiming to be a true medium, Houdini spent months investigating her. He quickly saw she was using magic; in fact, she used many tricks similar to ones he used in his career. He couldn't get others to agree with him, however, and made enemies over the Margery issue.

Margery grew to despise Houdini, threatening him through the "spirits." Eventually the magazine decided not to award her the prize, largely because of Houdini's vote against her. She never forgave him.

MR. HOUDINI GOES TO WASHINGTON

Houdini spent a lot of time and energy fighting the Spiritualists, hoping to put them out of business. He felt it was wrong to give people false hope that loved ones could contact them from the grave. Because he knew how magic illusions and

tricks were done, it made him furious that mediums used the tricks of professional magicians to cheat people.

One of the first books he read about magic when he was young was *Revelations of a Spirit Medium*. He used that information to prepare the mind-reading act he and Bess did for Dr. Hill's California Concert Company when they were first touring years before.

He knew it was a hoax then and soon quit doing the act, worried they had led people to believe things that weren't true.

After much bickering and many séances, no one won *Scientific American's* contest. But newspapers had been full of the story and sparked even more séances and public exhibitions by spirit mediums.

At the time, it was illegal in many states to perform fortune-telling for pay. In Washington, D.C., however, it was legal, and there were hundreds of mediums, astrologers, palm readers, and fortune-tellers in the nation's capital. Eventually, Houdini and others urged Congress to intervene and make it illegal for people to pretend to speak for the spirits of the dead or to charge money for fortune-telling in Washington, D.C. It was an effort to protect the public from frauds, but seemed to create even more interest in Spiritualism.

During four days of hearings before Congress in February and May 1926, Houdini matched wits with a crowd of astrologers, Spiritualists, mediums, and believers. Houdini showed members of Congress how mediums created illusions with trumpets and slate writing. In turn, the Spiritualists slapped insults at him, calling him names and saying anti-Jewish statements. One man, whose wife was a questionable medium, threatened to break Houdini's nose and tried to beat him, but a Congressman came between the two and stopped it.

During the hearings, it came out that several of the senators consulted mediums and astrologers. One senator's wife testified that in 35 years, she had not met a fake medium—all had been able to predict the future or get in touch with ghosts. Another senator's wife was a medium herself. Finally, a medium testified that even President Calvin Coolidge and his family held séances in the White House. The Coolidges had lost a son and perhaps were hoping to revive his spirit, like so many other grieving families who hired mediums. The Coolidges never spoke about the issue.

GHOSTS IN THE WHITE HOUSE

If the Coolidges were trying to speak to ghosts, they weren't the first or last in the White House to do so. President Pierce invited the Fox sisters to visit the White House, hoping to contact his dead son. Mary Lincoln invited mediums to hold séances several times to contact the Lincoln's young son, who died while Abraham Lincoln was president. More recently, President Ronald Reagan and his wife Nancy consulted a personal astrologer.

Ghosts are said to inhabit the White House, too. Many reports by employees, guests, and presidential families tell of encounters with ghosts of various presidents of the past.

During the four days of hearings, Houdini took insult after insult from the angry mediums and astrologers. They were angry he was out to destroy their careers. Even one of the senators insisted Houdini himself had spiritual powers he wouldn't admit. When the hearings were over, one of the angry mediums went up to Houdini and said, "You're a smart man, Mr. Houdini. But I can tell you something you don't know."

He was curious.

"I am waging war on the fraud mediums of this country." —HOUDINI

OUIJA BOARD

Ouija (pronounced WEE-jah or WEE-gee) boards first appeared in the mid-1800s, when Spiritualism began. It's not clear where the word *Ouija* came from. It's likely a made-up word, by the first person to get a patent for a talking board, Charles Kennard.

Talking boards were nothing new, however; they appeared in Ancient China and Greece. They were used to try to contact spirits by asking the board a question, then waiting for it to answer. In the 1920s the Ouija board was a popular tool for contacting psychic phenomena. People used it seriously, and as a fun fortune-telling toy, too.

Used around the world, Ouija boards are made by pasting a paper with words, letters, or numbers written on it to a smooth board. The planchette, the device that moves over the board, can be a saucer, coin, pen, or other object. Some of the first Ouija boards had a pencil fastened in the planchette that wrote out the answer on paper. Later, the board had the letters of the alphabet, numbers up to 10, and the words *yes* and *no* printed on it. The board would answer questions by moving the planchette to spell out answers or dates.

How did it work? The board didn't do anything, but the planchette *did* move, seemingly on its own, which made it a fascinating and fun experience. To use a Ouija board, everyone waited quietly, their fingers resting on the planchette, while someone asked the board a question. Then the planchette seemed to mysteriously move to spell out an answer or point to yes or no. It moved because of the ideo-motor effect, which means the players moved it without realizing it.

A talking board might write out a message.
MAGIC, ARNO PRESS, 1977 (REPRINT OF 1897 EDITION)

It's sort of like how our eyes create tears when we are sad—we don't tell the body to do it, it just happens. People didn't try to make the planchette move, but because they wanted it to, their bodies did it without their control. This made people think a spirit was moving their hands, and they thought the board had supernatural powers.

She said, "When November comes around, you won't be here."

He was puzzled.

"You'll be dead," she told him.

The next day, the newspapers carried stories about the revelation that President Coolidge consulted Spiritualists. The Coolidges never responded to the newspaper articles but members of Congress admitted they used fortune-tellers and spirit mediums frequently. There were hundreds of mediums listed in the newspaper ads in the Washington, D.C., area, so it was very possible.

Hearings continued in the Senate, even though the senator in charge of the bill was revealed to go to séances himself. After months of waiting, the bill never came up for a vote in Congress. The hearings were ignored. In fact, the records of the hearings were never published in the Congressional Record. Houdini had spent a lot of money, hiring private investigators and piecing together evidence to go after the criminals within Spiritualism, but it appeared they won the battle in Washington, D.C.

SPIRIT HANDS

To keep Spiritualism alive and interesting, mediums came up with new ideas to use

Houdini showed how to make wax hands, dipping his Vaseline-covered hand into warm paraffin.

in séances. Along with ectoplasm and spirit photographs, "spirit hands" were one of the new twists. In a séance, a medium could "catch" a ghost using a pan of hot water with melted paraffin in it. A séance group waited in the dark, then turned on the lights to reveal a mysterious handprint or footprint in the pan of wax. It was proof that a

Make a
Talking Board

Although Ouija boards are trademarked and sold by Parker Brothers today, talking boards have been around a long time and didn't always look like the ones sold in stores. You can make your own talking board like people did for years.

The planchette—the moving piece that spells out messages—was made from a piece of wood, sometimes with tiny wheels to move easily. Other items such as coins, a pen, a small saucer, or even a pendulum held on a chain over the board have also been used.

MATERIALS

Smooth, flat cardboard or old baking sheet, for the game board

Waterproof permanent markers

4-inch x 4-inch piece of heavy cardboard

Scissors

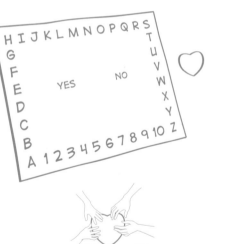

Prepare the board first, marking the letters of the alphabet, the numbers 1 through 10, and the words *yes* and *no*. There's no certain way they must appear on the board, but in alphabetical order and not overlapping is best.

Create the planchette by trimming the small cardboard piece to make a pointer shape, like a fat heart. Fingers will rest on the curved areas, so the pointed side can "select" the letters or numbers for the message.

Now, by yourself or with a friend, rest fingers lightly on the planchette and ask the board a question. See where it takes you, spelling out an answer, finding a number, or simply answering yes or no.

spirit had somehow been captured during the session.

Sometimes wax hands were found in the room, said to be left by a ghost. In one case, a fingerprint captured on a wax handprint during a séance was used to settle a $500,000 estate.

Houdini demonstrated how melted paraffin wax could easily be used to make handprints. After all, warm wax had been used in many ways by magicians. Some made fake hollow wax fingers to hide tiny items during a trick. Houdini also used a piece of wax to make an impression of a key to a jail cell or handcuffs, having a copy made later using the wax model.

While Houdini was working hard uncovering fraudulent mediums, he also feared their wrath. Several times he had been threatened. He made out a will, leaving his library of Spiritualist books to the American Society for Psychical Research and his vast collection of books and papers about magic to the Library of Congress. He left modest amounts of money to his assistants and left his estate in a trust to be divided among his brothers and sister. The rest of his assets, including the house, went to Bess.

His house was outfitted to keep track of visitors, as well as to impress and surprise them. When the front doorknob was turned, the door opened from the hinged side, due to hidden hinges on the side with the doorknob. Once inside, the house was full of hidden panels and passageways. Sometimes assistants would hide in another room, sliding open hidden panels to help Houdini do illusions and tricks for visitors. He also had the parlor wired to microphones that transmitted sound through a Dictaphone machine to a typist sitting in the basement. She would listen to the sounds and either type the messages out or reroute them to Houdini, who would be in another room of the house. He could listen in due to wire coils hidden beneath the carpeting that transmitted sound to a receiver belt he wore, attached to a telephone receiver he could hold in his hand.

He even hired an undercover spy of his own—a young magician named Amedeo Vacca. Houdini bought a barbershop down the street from his house, sent Vacca to barber school, and put him to work in the shop. When he needed to speak with Vacca, he visited the shop. No one knew the two were linked. Vacca was usually in the audience during Houdini's shows during this time, and he also inspected the stage and dressing rooms before performances.

THOMAS EDISON, GHOSTHUNTER

Thomas Edison, like many scientists at the time, tried to prove ghostly spirits actually existed. He was a practical thinker, believing that if something existed, it should be proven by scientific tests. He spent about 15 years working on experimental machines that could detect spirits of the dead, if they truly existed.

He created a photoelectric cell, similar to the kind used today to automatically turn on lightbulbs, such as nightlights, as the room darkens. Using a photoelectric cell, he aimed a beam of light directly at it. If anything crossed the path of the light, it would darken the light beam slightly, registering on a meter. Spirit mediums sat in the room and spent hours trying to summon ghosts. Despite repeated efforts, no spirits ever appeared and interrupted the light beam, triggering the sensitive needle to move on the meter.

Because the results of Edison's ghosthunting work were negative, he didn't reveal his discoveries. He knew many people continued to believe in ghosts, even wanted to, and he didn't want to disappoint them.

MODERN MECHANIX, OCTOBER 1933
Years later, this article about Edison's ghost trap invention was published. He used a light beam and meter to try to catch any paranormal spirits in the room. None appeared.

DICTAPHONE

The Dictaphone recorded sounds on a wax cylinder that could be played back at a slower speed. This made it possible for people to record things like business letters and messages that were typed out later by a person listening to the recording with headphones. The wax cylinder was replaced 50 years later by magnetic tape, like in tape recorders, and today dictating machines use hard drives to record and save sounds.

In this photo, a stenographer is typing up the message as she listens to it on headphones. In this case, she is blind, showing how useful such equipment can be.

Man speaking into a Dictaphone machine.

Typist listening to a recording on a Dictaphone.

He would install well-guarded secret equipment beforehand, too.

Houdini hired several women, including his beautiful young niece, to go undercover to séances, where they gathered information he planned to use in both his book and court cases against fraudulent mediums.

In Chicago, Spiritualists met to protest Houdini's criticisms of their activities. One claimed Houdini was crazy and belonged in an insane asylum. Others took out their rage in threats, hoping to scare Houdini off the project. In Boston, newspaper headlines blared "Houdini Gets Death Threat—'Evil Spirits' Put Curse on Him." He even received letters, threatening what the Spiritualists would do to him.

Houdini scoffed, claiming they didn't scare him because they had no power over him. "I am not denouncing Spiritualism, I am showing up the frauds," he pointed out. He challenged the Spiritualists to produce an honest medium who could actually contact a real spirit. Proof, he demanded. Solid, scientific, proof.

Their threats weren't idle. A friend of Houdini's who investigated fake mediums began carrying a gun after some phony mediums who had lost clients tried to kill him. There were rumors of mediums hiring thugs to beat up critics and using poison on enemies. To explain the violence, they blamed the spirits.

Houdini warned a friend to be careful and to avoid investigating alone. He was careful to send copies of all documents and investigation notes to his brother Hardeen for safekeeping in case anything happened to destroy the evidence he was building for a court case against fake mediums. He sometimes took assistant Amedeo Vacca with him when doing investigations. Houdini also disguised himself to better attend séances without attracting attention. He donned wigs, glasses, moustaches, and a variety of clothing to change his looks. Magnifying lenses in his eyeglasses helped him spot fraudulent tricks.

"Those mediums are bad actors and would think nothing of putting you in the hospital or worse," he told a friend.

In his battle against the frauds taking advantage of people through Spiritualism, Houdini published a book that revealed their tricks and secrets. He called it *A Magician Among the Spirits*. He rushed it into print, telling a friend, "I had a slight premonition that perhaps I would not live to see the book in print if I waited much longer."

Create Ghostly Handprints

hile melted wax can burn the skin if too hot, it's easy to see how imprints were made using plaster.

MATERIALS

Old newspapers

3 cups plaster of paris (sold at art and craft supply stores)

Empty paper milk carton (rinse out and open the top)

2 cups water

Paint-stirring stick (free at stores that sell paint)

Disposable aluminum pie plate

Vaseline or vegetable oil

Cover the work surface with newspapers. Put 3 cups of dry plaster into the milk carton. Slowly add the water, stirring with the stirring stick until all the powder dissolves.

When the mixture is smooth, pour it into the aluminum pie plate. Cover your hand with Vaseline or vegetable oil, and when the mixture begins to get solid, press your hand into the plaster. Hold it still for few minutes, then remove your hand.

It does seem to be magic, as the liquid turns to a solid, but it's due to a chemical reaction between the plaster and the water.

Was It Murder?

By 1926, at the age of 52, Houdini was ready to take it easy. He buried himself in his library, enjoying the days and nights filled with reading and researching the history of magic. He planned to write a new book about the history of superstition and witchcraft. He wanted to improve his writing ability, even get a college degree. He planned to enroll in a college English class as soon as his touring season was over.

MAGIC AS ART AND SCIENCE

Houdini wanted to make the field of magic a real profession, creating the first college of magic in the world. He discussed the possibility with members of the Society of American Magicians (SAM), which he had founded. Student magicians could take classes, pass exams, and receive a degree in magic. Classes such as History of Magic, Psychology of Magic, and courses in advertising and showmanship would be offered. He dreamed that through such a course, "magic, as an art and science, will be elevated to a higher level."

Houdini had many projects started, in the works, or at least on his mind. His focus was on magic—how to promote it, teach it, and create respect for it as a professional field. He had spent years trying to end the exploitation of magic techniques by the fake Spiritualists. He brought attention to the problem and created skepticism among the public. In doing so, he created the modern field of magic as entertainment, no longer any part of religious ceremonies or spirit powers. By fighting them, he had cleansed magic of the tawdry links to any special powers. Houdini demanded respect for the techniques and skills a good magic act required—not a hazy explanation of "special powers." For him, and magicians to follow, magic became an art and science. Success required talent and hard work. To claim any ability from an occult power was an insult to the profession.

Harry devoted his energy to cleaning up the Spiritualist frauds, both because it hurt the reputation of magicians and because they cheated innocent people. His book was out and gaining readers. Meanwhile, he continued his private investigations, gathering evidence to take fakes and phonies to court. The crusade cost money, however. Houdini had living expenses for himself and Bess, as well as salaries for several assistants, his personal librarian, and a bevy of people who worked undercover for him. He remained generous, too, giving money to those in need, and frequently giving away tickets to his shows, or doing free shows for hospitalized children.

He spent almost half a million dollars in today's money on investigations at that point. He needed to go back on the performance circuit from time to time, to earn enough money to continue the project.

FATAL BLOWS

While he hadn't come up with a sensational new act in several years, Harry continued doing short performances that focused on a few stage magic stunts and a lecture exposing Spiritualists. In September 1927 Harry and Bess set out for a five-month tour, beginning in Providence, Rhode Island, then going to the Midwest after a stop in Montreal, Canada. In Providence, Bess became very ill, with vomiting and a high fever. The Houdinis figured she had somehow gotten food poisoning, so she stayed in bed at the hotel. During Harry's Upside Down act, the cables fastened to the wooden piece holding his ankles were

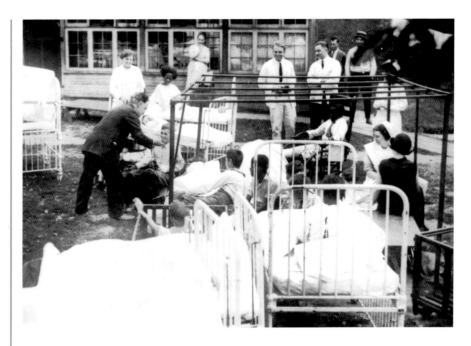

Houdini performed often for hospitalized children.
LIBRARY OF CONGRESS, LC USZ62-112408

127

twisted, and he ended up with a broken ankle. The doctor told him he was lucky— a bit more twist and his foot would have been sliced off by the accident. On crutches for days, he continued the tour wearing a splint and a leg brace.

On October 19 Harry gave a lecture against fake Spiritualists at McGill University in Montreal. The newspaper carried a story about it the next day, telling how he had attacked fake mediums who claimed to bring back dead loved ones. He was in pain from his ankle, lack of sleep, and caring for Bess, who was still not recovered. One person said he looked thin and tired, with dark circles under his eyes.

Three days later, a group of McGill students visited Houdini at his hotel. One muscular young man named J. Gordon Whitehead asked Houdini if it was true he could withstand punches to his stomach. Always proud of his physical fitness, in spite of his 52 years, Harry agreed, mostly to get the student to stop pestering him. Rather than throwing a simple punch, Whitehead launched a series of hard blows before Houdini could rise from the couch and tense his stomach muscles or brace himself against a chair. Later, while Houdini sat reading a newspaper in

the hotel lobby, a hefty stranger rushed up and punched him in the gut.

That evening after the show, he grew too weak to dress himself. A performance was scheduled for the next evening, in Detroit, Michigan. Early in the morning, when they boarded the train, Harry suffered such pain they wired ahead to have a doctor waiting when the train arrived in Detroit.

In Detroit, the doctor found Houdini in bad shape. He had a high fever, chills, and stomach pains. Determined to go on with the show that evening, he insisted on resting in a hotel instead of going to the hospital. That night, Houdini bravely carried on with the show, in spite of a very high fever and weakened condition. After the first act, he collapsed offstage. After reviving in the dressing room, he headed back to complete the show. Audience members remembered Houdini's efforts that night as clumsy and hoarse. His assistant had to help him complete a scarf act.

After midnight, Houdini's condition worsened. A doctor arrived, examined him, and insisted he come to the hospital. The next afternoon, surgeons opened his abdomen and removed his appendix. The internal bleeding and infection from the inflamed appendix filled his abdomen. The doctors warned he was near death.

Hoping to save his life, the doctors gave him a shot containing an experimental serum, created at a Detroit hospital. They refused to reveal what it contained. It brought his fever down a bit, and he was able to rest.

One young doctor tried to make Houdini as comfortable as possible. Harry began remembering his childhood back in Appleton as the doctor listened. "I sure would like some Farmer's Chop Suey again," Houdini told the doctor.

Farmer's Chop Suey had been a popular dish in Jewish homes, and Houdini was remembering his childhood as his health faded. The doctor went to a nearby deli and returned with a plate of Farmer's Chop Suey, which was a mixture of raw vegetables cut up and covered with sour cream. Houdini ate it slowly, remembering his early years.

"If I die, don't be surprised if phony Spiritualists declare a national holiday," he told the doctor.

A bit later the fever went back up, and he seemed to be going fast.

The next day, surgeons operated on him again. His condition steadily grew worse.

Farmer's Chop Suey

MATERIALS

Large bowl and mixing spoon

2 cups cottage cheese

1/2 cup plain yogurt or sour cream (sour cream salad dressing can be used, such as ranch dressings)

2 cups raw vegetables, chopped in pieces

Some to try: spinach, carrots, green beans, radishes, shredded lettuce, red cabbage, cherry tomatoes, green peppers, broccoli, cucumber

Mix the cottage cheese and yogurt or sour cream until blended. Add the chopped vegetables, and mix well.

You might simply want to use the cottage cheese/yogurt mixture as a dip, cutting the vegetables in larger pieces for dipping.

Houdini's brother Hardeen and widow Bess visit his grave.

Telegrams, flowers, and cards flooded into the hospital, urging Houdini to win the battle of his life. Bess, so upset over his condition, became ill again and had to be carried to his bedside for visits. During one of their brief visits, Houdini and Bess agreed that he would try to reach her from the grave if it was at all possible. He told her a secret phrase she would know was coming from him if he appeared as a ghost.

During a last visit with his brother Hardeen, Houdini told him, "I can't fight anymore."

Houdini died at Grace Hospital in Detroit the afternoon of October 31.

It was Halloween—the Spiritualists' national holiday.

His body was placed in a bronze coffin, draped with flowers, and sent by railcar to New York for burial. About 2,000 mourners packed his funeral, with about as many crowding the street outside the Elks Clubhouse near Times Square. Thousands of flowers and tributes surrounded the casket. A representative of Houdini's beloved Society of American Magicians began a tradition by breaking a wooden magician's wand and laying it on Houdini's casket. The tradition continues to this day, commemorating the death of a fellow magician.

QUESTIONS REMAIN

Meanwhile, a grieving public directed their suspicions at the Detroit doctors. Experts insisted that stomach punches couldn't cause appendicitis because it is the result of bacterial infection. Others said the doctors were too quick to use surgery and were wrong to try an unknown experimental drug. Newspapers called it a crime and demanded an investigation.

For more than 80 years, people have wondered if foul play—not a burst appendix—felled the nation's "superman."

Houdini's body was buried quickly in Queens, New York, in a cemetery he had chosen years earlier. There was no medical examination or autopsy done of his body after it left the hospital. The death certificate listed his cause of death as complications from a ruptured appendix.

But it wasn't so simple. Questions immediately arose. Within days newspaper headlines read "Was Houdini Murdered?" Houdini had led such a superhuman life, it was hard to accept that he was dead at such a young age and so quickly. But the questions kept coming—he'd been given an experimental serum in an injection at the hospital. What was it, and who ordered it? Was it poison? The death certificate listed his appendix as being on his left side— appendixes are located in the lower right abdomen. And, the idea that appendicitis could be caused by a stomach punch doesn't seem medically possible.

The second man to punch Houdini, the unknown attacker in the hotel lobby, was later discovered to be a friend of a prominent government official's wife who strongly believed in the occult and Spiritualism.

In his will, Harry had left all his magic equipment to his brother Hardeen, who resumed his career as a magician, using some of Harry's acts. In no time he received death threats, and the Ritz Hotel even asked for police protection for Hardeen while he was their guest. It's not clear why anyone wanted to kill Hardeen; perhaps it was because they suspected he had also inherited Houdini's files of investigations about fake mediums.

In London, a man who had helped Houdini in one of his investigations reported to police that someone had broken into his home and slashed a painting Houdini had given him as a gift years before.

After his home was broken into and some of Harry's old equipment stolen, Hardeen burned all of Harry's files.

Bess was heartbroken after Harry's death. She and Harry had been a very close couple. They had actually created a secret code, promising that whoever died first would try to contact the other from the afterworld. Their secret code was "Rosabelle, believe." It came from the song Bess had been singing in the Floral Sisters act when she and Harry first met. The first line went "Rosabelle, sweet Rosabelle, I love you more than I can tell." After waiting beside Harry's photograph every Sunday for months after his death, Bess gave up trying to contact him.

"My last hope is gone," she said. "It is finished. Good night, Harry!"

Eventually Bess tried returning to show business but was never successful without Harry. She followed Harry's wishes, donating his papers and large collection of magic research materials to the Library of Congress so the public could use them. After paying debts she was comfortable, but not a wealthy woman. Years later she married again, settling into a life without public attention. Bess Houdini died in 1943.

DIGGING UP HOUDINI?

Scientists and family members may go ahead with exhuming Houdini's remains—digging up his bones—to see if any answers can be found to the many questions behind his mysterious death. An exhumation is no easy matter—it's illegal to simply dig up someone's long-dead body. George Hardeen, grandson of Harry's brother Theo, wants to go ahead with the process. "It needs to be looked at," he said. "His death shocked the entire nation, if not the world. Now maybe it's time to take a second look."

An attorney has filed legal papers with the city of New York to proceed. Dr. James Starrs, an expert pathologist who has worked on many unsolved deaths, may analyze Houdini's remains. "Everything will be thoroughly analyzed," Starrs said. "We'll examine his hairs, his fingernails, any bone fractures."

What exactly can scientists discover by looking at Houdini's bones? Right after his death, the theory that he was poisoned, likely by arsenic, appeared. All bones contain some arsenic, but high levels would indicate he was likely victim of a cruel murder plot. If not arsenic, there's still the question of whether he was poisoned with the experimental serum he was injected with by one of his doctors at the Detroit hospital.

Even one of Margery's great grandchildren wants to go ahead with the study. "If there's any circumstantial evidence Houdini was poisoned, we have to explore that," she said.

But descendants of Bess Houdini's family resist the idea. They claim it's a publicity stunt and plan to fight any efforts to dig up Houdini's remains.

If Houdini's death was a plot by Spiritualists, the proof remains to be found. Houdini, always mysterious, may have taken his biggest secret to his grave. We may never really know what killed him.

RESOURCES

FURTHER READING

Books by Harry Houdini

1906 *The Right Way to Do Wrong: An Exposé of Successful Criminals*

1908 *The Unmasking of Robert-Houdin*

1910 *Handcuff Secrets Exposed*

1920 *Magical Rope Ties and Escapes*

1920 *The Miracle Mongers and Their Methods*

1922 *Houdini's Paper Magic*

1924 *A Magician Among the Spirits*

Books About Harry Houdini

Escape! The Story of the Great Houdini by Sid Fleischman. Greenwillow.

Harry Houdini: Death-Defying Showman by Rita Mullin. Sterling Biographies Series.

Harry Houdini by Vicki Cobb. DK Biography Series.

Harry Houdini: A Magical Life by Elizabeth MacLeod. Kids Can Press.

Houdini: Master of Illusion by Clinton Cox. Scholastic.

Spellbinder: The Life of Harry Houdini by Tom Lalicki. Holiday House.

Who Was Harry Houdini? by Tui T. Sutherland. Grosset and Dunlap.

Magic Books

Magic Science by Jim Wiese. Scholastic.

My Magic Book by Dennis Patten. Western Publishing Company.

Self-Working Table Magic: 97 Foolproof Tricks with Everyday Objects by Karl Fulves. Dover Publications.

Usborne Book of Magic Tricks by Rebecca Heddle and Ian Keable. EDC Publishing.

WEB SITES TO EXPLORE

Houdini in the *New York Times*
www.houdinimuseum.org
This site has online stories and news coverage about Harry Houdini that appeared in the *New York Times*.

Houdini: The Man Behind the Myth
www.pbs.org/wgbh/amex/houdini
Public television's American Experience series program site for the film, *Houdini: The Man Behind the Myth.* You can view clips from Houdini's movies at this site.

Houdini Photographs
http://memory.loc.gov/ammem/vshtml/vshdini.html
This is the Library of Congress Web site. There are digitized photographs of Houdini from between 1886 to 1926. To find it from the library's main page at

www.loc.gov, search for "Variety Stage," then click on "Variety Stage." That will take you to "Houdini." Bess left Harry's large collection of books and photos to the Library of Congress, just as Harry had wanted.

Harry Houdini: Selected Resources from the Appleton Public Library.

www.apl.org/history/Houdini/index.html
The Appleton, Wisconsin, library maintains a collection of Houdiniana.

The Castle Museum

www.foxvalleyhistory.org
This is a local history museum called The Castle, in Appleton, Wisconsin. They have a large collection of Houdini materials and have an online exhibit.

AKA Houdini

www.akahoudini.org
This Web site is the online version of the exhibit at the Fox Valley History Society museum in Appleton, Wisconsin. AKA Houdini has lots of images, facts, and games.

Magic Tricks

www.magictricks.com/houdini/bio.htm
Lots of interesting information about magic, as well as Houdini information. This site tells how some popular magic tricks are done.

Conjuring Arts Research Center

www.conjuringarts.org
This site is full of information, including access to a database of all Houdini research used by the authors of the book, *Houdini: The Making of America's First Superhero*.

SOURCES

Ashby, LeRoy. *With Amusement for All: A History of American Popular Culture Since 1830*. Lexington, KY: University Press of Kentucky, 2005.

Bell, Don. *The Man Who Killed Houdini*. Montreal: Vehicule Press, 2005.

Brandon, Ruth. *The Life and Many Deaths of Harry Houdini*. New York: Random House, 1993.

Christopher, Milbourne and Maurine. *The Illustrated History of Magic*. New York: Carroll and Graf Publishers, 2006.

Gibson, Walter. *Houdini's Escapes and Magic*. New York: Blue Ribbon Books, reprint 1976 by Funk and Wagnalls.

Gibson, Walter B., and Morris N. Young, ed. *Houdini on Magic*. New York: Dover Publications, 1953.

Hoffman, Professor. *Hoffmann's Modern Magic*. New York: Dover Publications, 1978 (reprint of 1876 edition).

Hopkins, Albert A. *Magic: Stage Illusions and Scientific Diversions, Including Trick Photography*. New York: Arno Press, 1977 (reprint of 1897 edition).

Houdini, Harry. *Houdini's Paper Magic*. Netherlands: Fredonia Books, 2001 (reprint of Houdini's 1922 book).

Houdini, Harry. *The Miracle Mongers and Their Methods*. Hard Press, 2007 (reprint of 1918 book).

Houdini, Harry. *The Right Way to Do Wrong: An Exposé of Successful Criminals*. New York: Cosimo, Inc., 2007 (reprint of 1906 book).

Kalush, William, and Larry Sloman, *The Secret Life of Houdini: The Making of America's First Superhero*. New York: Atria Books, 2006.

Silverman, Kenneth. *Houdini!!! The Career of Ehrich Weiss*. New York: Harpercollins, 1996.

INDEX